"I am Alvin Ailey. I am a choreographer. I am a black man whose roots are in the sun and dirt of the south. My roots are in the blues, in the street people whose lives are full of beauty and misery and pain and hope. My roots are also in the Gospel church, the Gospel church of the south where I grew up. Holy blues, paeons to joy, anthems to the human spirit."

*Choreography and Dance*, 1996, Vol 4(1), pp. 1–7

# Alvin Ailey: Signposts of an American Visionary

C. S'thembile West

During its three and a half decades, the Alvin Ailey Company has left lasting markers on the playing field of American Modern Dance. It has established a reputation for precise but spectacular dancing, for depicting an African American ethos with sensitivity and elegance, and set standards for performance excellence. Ailey's choreography caused shock waves in the dance world of 1958 and continues to move audiences deeply. The company has also provided a paradigm for a modern dance repertory company.

KEY WORDS   *Revelations*; Blues; American Modern Dance

1993. The Alvin Ailey American Dance Theater turns thirty-five. During these three decades, the Ailey Company has left lasting markers on the playing field of American Modern Dance. Long before Mr Ailey passed on, December 1st, 1989, the company had established a reputation for precise but spectacular dancing, for depicting an African American ethos with sensitivity and elegance, showcasing works of new and established choreographers, along with setting standards for performance excellence. Hence, the Ailey legacy is as diverse as the eclectic repertory danced by company members. And although Mr Ailey himself is no longer at the helm of the Ailey Company, the patterns that he established have become benchmarks of American modern dance.

In a 1983 *New York Times* review, Anna Kisselgoff appropriately referred to the Alvin Ailey American Dance Theater not as a company, but a "school of thought." In a company in which choreographer and dancers turned history into a sensibility, solo performance into a ritual and going to a dance concert like going to the movies, new ground was forever being broken. In fact, since the performance of *Blues Suite* in Mr Ailey's first full-scale concert in 1958 at the Theresa Kaufman Auditorium of the Ninety-second Street YMHA, where he had first presented work in March of that same year, Alvin Ailey has become a household word in U.S. modern dance.

Alvin Ailey's choreographic genius upset the dance world of 1958. *Blues Suite* is a telling distillation of powerful human emotions told through one lens of Black life in a small town where night and molded dreams are eased by sexuality. Despite its setting, *Blues Suite* speaks to emotions felt by all human beings who know the pain of loss, heartache, defeat and triumph. The classic blues score that accompanies the ballet roots it in African America, just as strongly as it roots the emotions depicted there. Time-crusted memories eased through the cracks of broken-dreams and heartfelt anguish. Rememberings of love-filled moments, as

The reproduction of this article is courtesy of the American Dance Festival. The article appears in its 1988 publication *African American Genius in Modern Dance*.

well as tender embraces of love's caring, oozes through *Blues Suite*. Frothy blues lyrics and riffs of melancholy haunt *Good Morning Blues*, which Jimmy Rushing made famous in the 1940s.

Full-bodied movement sequences, reminiscent of Lester Horton's laterals and long low lunges, defiant cadences and tough-minded panache make *Blues Suite* not only striking and palatable, but also kinesthetically familiar to diverse audiences. It is perhaps to our advantage that Mr Ailey experienced a consummate theatrical apprenticeship along with his own first company members Carmen de Lavallade, James Truitte and Joyce Trisler, in the Lester Horton Dance Theater, Hollywood, California. In fact, when Horton died in 1953, Alvin and Frank Eng were essential to Dance Theater's survival until 1960. In an interview by Moria Hodgson in *Dance News*, April 1976, Mr Ailey had this to say about his mentor: "Lester Horton was the greatest influence of my career. He is the reason I do all this. He was a genius at the theater. Besides being a major choreographer he was a master costume designer, master painter, master sculptor. An incredible man . . . When you came into the world of Lester Horton you came into a completely creative environment – people of all colors, music of all nations. . . ." Clearly, Mr Ailey's own company is a reflection of this strong Horton influence. Mr Ailey's works have indeed always been theatrical masterpieces, dramatic collages of music, sets, costuming, lights and gesticular drama, hence consummate, enthralling theater.

At the same time the people of Ailey's ballets look like people, blues people, solo people, group people, people we all know. The bear resemblance to a time and space shared by a proverbial everyman: pain and joy. Yet, they are inevitably Black people. People who inhabit a Black world with sensitivities that are portrayed in a distinctively ethnic way, with a cultural relativity that bespeaks Africa and African America, yet touches a nerve in everyone. The Ailey language is a universal language. Hence, when his dancers move, they are understood not only aesthetically, that is, as carriers of notions of what is beautiful and pleasing, but also viscerally. Ailey dancers have a sock-it to 'em, hit-'em-in-the-gut kind of attack and panache. They pack a wallop, pure and simple.

An "Ailey dancer" is as important to Ailey's choreography as the patterns themselves. In fact, when a critic comments that such and such a dancer looks like an "Ailey dancer," the implication is that that dancer moves with strength, employs dramatic tension and is technically proficient. In other words, over three decades Ailey dancing has come to mean consummate performance.

This well-deserved reputation for excellence in performance has set a standard of performance which is obvious in other modern dance companies that have formed since the sixties. The Ailey influence is particularly evident in African American modern dance companies like the Philadelphia Dance Company (PDC), affectionately called Philadanco, and the Dayton Contemporary Dance Company (DCDC).

That Ailey look is apparent in the impeccable technical facility of the dancers and the bravura of their performance styles. Their look and feel resemble the Ailey Company. But more importantly, the smoothness of delivery, the seamless packaging of concert staples (i.e. sets, costumes, lights), in addition to the well integrated repertory, make both the Dayton and Philadelphia companies keepers of that Ailey performance legacy. They are proof that Ailey did indeed provide a model of performance excellence. These contemporary aestheticians move proudly within a framework modelled by the Alvin Ailey American Dance Theater, a

**Figure 2**   James Truitte in "I Want To Be Ready" from *Revelations*.

model marked by a pyrotechnical facility and dramatic flare that allows them to finesse every possible choreographic pitfall.

On another note, both the Dayton Contemporary Dance Company, founded in 1968, and the Philadelphia Dance Company, established in 1970, like the Ailey Company, were created to provide not only high quality dance, but also dance that reflects a Black experience. Critical notes on the DCDC emphasize that "as a modern dance company rooted in the African American experience, it is DCDC's mission to deliver contemporary dance of the highest quality to the broadest possible audience." These objectives sound almost exactly like Alvin's rationale for establishing his own company ten years earlier: to demonstrate aspects of African America while providing quality, entertaining theater. The Ailey model looms large in contemporary modern dance.

Like the Ailey Company, many of today's younger modern dance companies perform the works of itinerant choreographers and dancers. Like Ailey, who believed that "Modern dance will die if we don't do each other's work" (*Philadelphia Inquirer*: December 12, 1989), Joan Myers Brown, Jeraldyne Blunden, Cleo Parker Robinson, artistic directors of DPC, DCDC and the Cleo Parker Robinson Dance Company in Denver respectively, provide opportunities for new as well as established choreographers to set works on their dancers. The AAADT provides a choreographic home for works by outstanding Black dancemakers like

Talley Beatty, Katherine Dunham, Louis Johnson, Donald McKayle, Eleo Pomare, Pearl Primus and Billy Wilson. The company also provides younger, contemporary choreographers like Dianne McIntyre of the now disbanded Sounds in Motion Dance Company, Kevin Wynn, director of The Kevin Wynn Collection, Donald Byrd of Donald Byrd and The Group, Bill T. Jones and Jawole Zollar, director of Urban Bush Women, with opportunities to expose their work to larger audiences. Over three decades of commissioned works, revivals and reconstructions of dances by African American dancemakers, the Ailey Company has helped to preserve precious choreographic gems. In salvaging and preserving repertory works from African America, Alvin functioned as a curator, not only of dance, but also of the voices that articulate issues of artistic, social and cultural concern to African Americans. In commissioning the works of new Black dancemakers, Alvin fostered and expanded the boundaries of American Modern Dance and "stood as [a] bulwark against the ephemerality of dance" (*Philadelphia Inquirer*: December 24, 1989).

On the other hand the Ailey Company's repertory has always included ballets by notable and not so notable choreographers of European ancestry. Works by John Butler, Lester Horton, Lucas Hoving, Pauline Koner, Joyce Trisler, Paul Sanasardo and Anna Sokolow found homes in the repertory of the AAADT in the sixties, while dances by Louis Falco, Lar Lubovitch, Jennifer Muller and Rudy Perez became part of the Ailey collection in the seventies. By the eighties choreography by Choo San Goh, Elisa Monte and Kathryn Posin had added their voices to the AAADT repertory. Hence, the Ailey Company proved to be a truly American company, representing distinctive voices within American dance, thereby making the AAADT a model of harmony within diversity. The Ailey Company demonstrates that the American experiment, that dream of unity and equality for which Martin Luther King, Jr. sacrificed his life is, indeed, possible.

In order to contextualize Ailey dancers within the framework of U.S. modern dance, we need to look at the profile of a modern dancer and then at what there is about Alvin Ailey's dancers that have expanded the boundaries of American Modern Dance over the years. In the tradition of dance pioneers Isadora Duncan, Ruth St. Denis and Ted Shawn, who were shaped by the socio-historical events of their time, Alvin Ailey came to voice at a time when the socio-political climate for Black people in the U.S. was encouraging and hopeful. The 1954 legislative ruling in Brown vs. the Topeka Board of Education, which declared that separate schools for Blacks and Whites were inherently unequal, was but four years old when Ailey formed his company. Martin Luther King, Jr. had been elected president of the Southern Christian Leadership Conference in 1957. And in 1959, when AAADT was a mere year old, Edward Kennedy [Duke] Ellington received the Spingarn Medal, which Ailey himself would receive later. So a sense of hope, rejuvenation and the reaffirmation of possibilities for change were pervasive among African Americans when Alvin began his company.

In the previous decades two European World Wars and the Korean conflict, in which thousands of African Americans lost their lives securing 'peace and justice' abroad, had galvanized a distinctly African American thrust for self-determination through economic and political strategies. The Civil Rights Movement was gaining momentum with grassroots organizations giving voice to African American needs and aspirations particularly in the South. Black Church organizations were solidifying black political power in urban areas like Philadelphia, Detroit and

Chicago, as well as in places like Atlanta and Albany, Georgia, Memphis and Birmingham. These thrusts gave voice to the heretofore limited voice of African Americans. Alvin Ailey's entry into this sweep of historical events impacted upon the themes Alvin selected and the reception he received upon entry onto the stage of American Modern Dance.

**Figure 3** Alvin Ailey and Carmen de Lavallade in Ailey's *Roots of the Blues*, Jacob's Pillow, 1961. Photo by John Lindquist.

Ailey's choreography took the bare bones sentimentality of the blues, a blues associated with a legacy of African disenfranchisement on American (U.S.) shores, mixed it with victorious attitudinal stances and created the ballet, *Blues Suite*, that pulled and tugged at the chords of human emotion. Escaping the magnetic pull of the blues danced Ailey style, was rare, if not impossible. No one was exempt from the pull of Ailey's choreographic magnetism. It was this magnetic quality that mesmerized the dance world of 1958 and set in motion a series of events that proceeded to transform the world of American (U.S.) Modern Dance.

The texture of down home, rich, Southern Blues with a twist of Texas, Ailey's state of origin, forms the vortex of Alvin's sensibility. A blues vocabulary that speaks to work-a-day logic and ethos with a spirituality which articulates that everything is indeed all right in the universe, comprises that magnetic component of Mr Ailey's choreography, thereby creating a consistent voice of protest and concern. Human beings, black, bold and triumphant, doing right by themselves and others, in spite of hindrances, are the focus of Ailey's ballets. But unlike any other company of his time, Ailey took the rich, earth-toned, pulsating electricity of African American hope and perseverance, as demonstrated in sure-fired gaits, adamant stances and who-you-think-you-talkin'-to insinuations and attitudes, and mixed them into a batter that revolutionized the world of American (U.S.) Modern Dance. Alvin Ailey's ballets, *Revelations* (1960), *Roots of the Blues* (1961), *Masekela Langage* (1969) and *Cry* (1971), like that first highly acclaimed ballet, *Blues Suite* (1958), consistently speak to the core of human existence.

The modern dance lexicon would be sorely lacking if the choreographic genius of Alvin Ailey were omitted, but more importantly, to overlook the fact that Mr Ailey's work set standards not only for performance excellence, but also for choreography, costume design, make-up artistry and deportment, would be to miss the eclectic range of his contributions to American (U.S.) dance theater.

Yes, Mr Ailey's choreographic inventiveness caused shock waves in the dance world of 1958 when he presented his first concert in New York. *Blues Suite* marked the beginning of an illustrious choreographic career. *Blues Suite* was a quintessential work because it moved beyond sultry bordello images and touched spots deep within the souls of those who watched it. *Blues Suite*, like the radiant masterwork, *Revelations*, touches pain and desire and souls.

In fact, audiences are still so deeply moved by *Revelations* that they continually rise from their seats as if to wrap themselves more intimately in the revivalist euphoria of the "Rock'a My Soul" section. Mr Ailey's choreography for *Revelations* continues to mesmerize thousands of dance aficionados, children and adults from every imaginable background, as he offers them slices of African American sensibility. Hence, Alvin created a universal language of emotion palatable to diverse ethnic groups.

Ailey was a multiculturalist long before the term gained national parlance. He selected dancers not for their color, but for the verve, bravura and acumen of their performance. Although the majority of Ailey company members have been and continue to hail from the ranks of African American, Tina Yuan, Masazumi Chaya, Mari Kajiwara, Linda Kent, Maxine Sherman, Peter Woodin, Michihiko Oka, Jodi Moccia, et al., demonstrate that the Ailey touch did indeed inspire and draw dancers from diverse disciplines and cultural backgrounds.

Ailey was a renaissance man, a humanist, consciously selecting, reshaping and transforming concepts and ideas, so that the thrust of his messages would, indeed, be accessible to masses, regardless of age or cultural heritage. In the small town of Rogers, Texas, forty miles northeast of Austin and approximately 140 miles northwest of Houston, where the True Vine Baptist Church, gospel choirs, fiery preaching and clientele at the Dew Drop Inn were continual presences, Ailey's choreographic voice was shaped and influenced. Those experiences rooted Ailey in a tradition rich not only in creative endurance and triumph over seemingly insurmountable odds, but in a legacy of synthesis and transformation. Since the period of enslavement, African Americans have become masters of making something out of nothing. Hence, it was not surprising that Alvin Ailey, one of many from simple roots, rose to prominence in a society that made no special efforts to include him. Like Helmsley Winfield in the thirties and Katherine Dunham in the forties, Alvin Ailey widened, expanded and opened more doors for black performers on the concert stage since 1958. Alvin provided inspiration and opportunity for generations of dancers and grounded them in the historical reality of African America. Alvin led them to a beauty inside themselves as he exposed them to the beauty of an American legacy powerfully shaped by an African presence.

Mr Ailey's dances chronicle the cultural and historical matrix of the United States, as they signal African American sensibilities and concerns. Alvin Ailey's ballets, as a voice in an orchestra of ethnic diversity, speak to the ever changing landscape of modern dance in the U.S. Hence, the legacy of Alvin Ailey represents that which is distinctly American at the same time that it is uniquely African American.

Perhaps Alvin's most memorable piece, *Revelations*, often referred to as his signature work, contains the essential idiomatic and axiomatic expressions of African American history. Created to commemorate Alvin's roots, *Revelations* is testimony to the endurance and adaptability of people of African descent in the U.S. Although *Revelations* is often viewed as a dance drama of elegance and sophistication framing African American motifs in an artistic mode, the ballet is an icon that stands as a signpost of the victorious thoughts and survival mechanisms that enabled enslaved Africans to keep their minds on freedom.

The lexicon of American Modern Dance would be incomplete without inclusion of the choreographic inventiveness of Alvin Ailey. The Alvin Ailey American Dance Theater, introduced to the world of performance in 1958, launched a new chapter in the annals of theatricality. His dances chronicle not only the cultural and historical concerns of African Americans, as they demonstrate African American sensibilities, but also speak to the changing landscape of modern dance in the U.S. Alvin Ailey's choreographic text is like the rhythm section of a band that keeps the heart of the thing alive. His voice is the pulse of America. It is the articulation of the meaning and power of relationships, life and living in the U.S. It is the voice of America.

For more than three decades now the dances of Alvin Ailey have been strategic signposts marking the triumph of the human spirit. As totems of victorious thought, that is, creating viable spaces out of near nothingness, Ailey's dances from *Blues Suite* (1958) to *Opus McShann* (1989) have not only celebrated historic chapters in African American history, but have also concisely captured human emotion and sentiment. He has achieved this with a panache, skill and sophistication that has affected a metamorphosis in American Modern Dance. This Ailey-infused transformation of modern dance has impacted companies, critics, dancers, dance teachers and audiences. Hence, that unique Ailey approach and style, which I have attempted to define in this article, survives his tenure, and thereby provides a model for quality performance. The AAADT demonstrates the standards of performance to be emulated by choreographers and dancers, as American Modern Dance and the Alvin Ailey American Dance Theater, with Judith Jamison at the helm, move triumphantly into the twenty-first century.

*Choreography and Dance*, 1996, Vol 4(1), pp. 9–12
Photocopying permitted by license only

**Figure 4**   James Truitte and Minnie Marshall in "Fix Me, Jesus" from *Revelations*.

# Dear Alvin

## James Truitte

Alvin Ailey's life is a lesson in how to make beauty with a buzz (saw). How Ailey "got that way" goes back to his encounters with Lester Horton and with Horton's pupils Carmen de Lavallade and the author. Dance history was made excruciatingly painful but, in retrospect, worth it by this twentieth century Mercury.

KEY WORDS   Carmen de Lavallade; Lester Horton

It is sometimes very difficult to take pen in hand to write about as close and revered a friend as was Alvin Ailey. He was one of the most complex, unpredictable, brooding, indecisive and, at times, one of the most animated persons who lived on this earth. Being a friend to Alvin was a constant challenge, for you never knew which complexity or personality you would encounter from day to day.

Our association began at the Lester Horton Theater and School in Los Angeles. Had it not been for Alvin's seeing Jack Cole's fantastic choreography for *Down to Earth*, starring Rita Hayworth – had it not been for his close friend Carmen de Lavallade introducing him to Lester Horton, the dance world would never have had the opportunity to experience this creative genius who, like Joseph, wore a coat of many colors. Alvin's qualities became apparent, triggered by his appearance, disappearance, and reappearance at the Horton School. His intermittent appearances did, however, allow him to profit from Horton's theatricality: his lighting, costume design, and use of color. By 1954, Alvin had all this information safely tucked in his pocket when, after Horton's death in 1953 and Ailey's interim serving as resident choreographer for the company, he and de Lavallade left Los Angeles to dance in the Broadway show *House of Flowers*.

Four years later, in 1958, when he was returning from a Mexican vacation, Alvin stopped in Los Angeles to visit family and pay a call on the Horton brood. Our season was in production and Alvin was very pleased that we had maintained the company and were carrying on in the tradition of our mentor Horton.

In 1960, as a John Hay Whitney Fellow, I arrived in New York to study Labanotation at the Dance Notation Bureau in order to notate the Horton Technique. At that time Alvin was preparing for another concert at the Ninety-second Street YW/YMHA; the first had been in 1958. He asked me to appear. This was the concert which featured the premiere of *Revelations*, all 45 minutes of it! Knowing when to stop was not one of Alvin's talents. Some months later he formed his first permanent company of five members: Minnie Marshall, Ella Thompson Moore, Myrna White, Alvin and me. We were awarded space at the YWCA at Fifty-first Street and 8th Avenue through the efforts of Charlie Blackwell and Executive Director Edele Holtz. Out of this sprang that wonderful, exciting and creative hub, the Clark Center.

This relationship afforded Alvin the initial opportunity to present the Alvin Ailey American Dance Theater with Carmen de Lavallade as guest artist. Recognition and success followed; the rest is history.

I have been troubled over the years about why Alvin didn't incorporate the black experience into more of his work, as was his original intention. The scenarios he envisioned were monumental and unfortunately many never developed. It would have been interesting to see how he would have created works about Henri Christophe, Touissant L'Ouverture, Harriet Tubman et al. In retrospect, he did do this by giving opportunities to other black choreographers: Talley Beatty, Donald McKayle, Louis Johnson, Geoffrey Holder, and, on the white side, John Butler and Anna Sokolow.

After we returned from our 1962 State Department sponsored tour, Alvin completely dropped from the repertoire a stunning piece by Glen Tetley entitled *Mountainway Chant*, based on Native American culture which I believe would have been a vital piece for all time. In spite of such lapses, Alvin acquired one of the most eclectic repertoires in the dance world.

**Figure 5**  James Truitte and Carmen de Lavallade in Lester Horton's *The Beloved.*

I departed from the company in 1968. I felt that, in his later years, except for a few good pieces, his creative flame was dying. Very few of us knew that he could not create a piece at the drop of a hat, a new work for every season.

Alvin, I thank you from the bottom of my heart for the last eight years of my dancing career. I thank you for giving me national and international recognition, and for taking me around the world two and a half times – an experience anyone would savor.

In spite of the many dastardly things you did to many dancers and to me in particular, I have forgiven and forgotten. Many of these problems could have been handled if you had been able to confront the issues. Facing any kind of confrontation was not one of your outstanding attributes, particularly when it was you who'd created the turmoil. I know we would have accepted any decision if it had come directly from you instead of from someone else less respected.

I am thankful that our friendship withstood the good, bad and indifferent. Alvin, you will always have a very special place in my heart. If you can read this from above, while choreographing for the angels, I know you will give it your stamp of approval for the truth is the light.

You are a true friend, when you accept all the facets, negative and positive. Objectively, I have.

**Figure 6**   James Truitte as the Eagle Man with Alvin Ailey and Carmen de Lavallade in Glen Tetley's *Mountainway Chant.*

*Choreography and Dance*, 1996, Vol 4(1), pp. 13–20
Photocopying permitted by license only

# An Inside View of the Alvin Ailey American Dance Theater

Muriel Topaz

Based on a conversation with Dudley Williams, the article traces a short history of the company through the eyes of one of its long time soloists. Williams discusses what it was like to work with Alvin Ailey from the time of his joining the company in the early 1960s through Ailey's untimely death in 1988.

KEY WORDS   Dudley Williams, *Revelations*, *Blues Suite*, Judith Jamison

The following article is an account of a conversation in the library of the Alvin Ailey American Dance Center on July 27, 1994.*

Dudley Williams, as intense, voluble and commanding in person as he is on stage, has been with the Alvin Ailey American Dance Theater continuously for thirty years. That is, possibly, a world's record for any dancer with any company; it certainly is a record for the Ailey company. His reminiscences about the company and about his dear friend Alvin give, perhaps, the very best picture of how the company formed and how it grew.

When he was twelve years old Dudley started studying both ballet and modern dance with Sheldon Hoskins at The School on the Hill at 145th Street in New York City. Despite these early, somewhat erratic dance studies, Williams maintains that he became a dancer by accident; he was really headed for a career as a concert pianist. When he auditioned for the High School of Performing Arts (HSPA), there were no more openings for musicians and he was asked "do you do anything else?" That's how he happened to audition as a dancer. He entered HSPA with the idea of switching to music as soon as there was an opening; the switch never happened.

HSPA was followed by two years at the Juilliard School where he, along with fellow students William Louther and Mabel Robinson, were spotted by Martha Graham. A scholarship to study at the Graham school was offered and accepted.

During his high school years Williams was already performing as a professional in the companies of Hava Kohav, May O'Donnell and Eleo Pomare. While at Juilliard he continued his performing career with Donald McKayle and Talley Beatty, and danced at the Spoleto Festival in Italy.

Thinking that he was well prepared by having studied with Antony Tudor, Karel Shook, May O'Donnell and Martha Graham, and by having had a good deal of performing experience, he auditioned for a series of Broadway shows. "It was then I found out about the cruel dance world," said Williams. "I never made an audition because I couldn't sing."

---

* Other sources consulted by the author include *Alvin Ailey American Dance Theater,* a pamphlet about the company written by Laura Beaumont and various articles in *Dance Magazine, Dance News,* and *Ballet International.*

In the meanwhile, in 1958, Ailey had founded his company, the Alvin Ailey American Dance Theater. With a friend, Ernest Parham, he had gathered together thirty-five dancers and gave eight concerts in the Ninety-second Street YMHA in New York. They performed *Blues Suite*, some Latin dances and a solo dedicated to Lester Horton that Ailey, himself, danced. Those first concerts were an immediate success.

In 1961, Williams had been invited to join the Graham company and toured with it through 1962. At the end of the tour, he was "let go" as there was no more work. After staying in Germany for a bit, he decided to return to the United States, give up dancing and attend college. Just before he was to enroll, Ailey, an avid dance concert goer who had seen Williams perform, called and said "Dudley, I need you."

For seven years Williams danced with both the Martha Graham Company and the Alvin Ailey American Dance Theater. Since neither of the two companies worked all of the time, and since both toured much of the same circuit, for those seven years their schedules didn't conflict. When schedule conflicts finally became a problem, Williams had little difficulty in choosing the Ailey company. Said Williams, "Martha was Biblical, archaic; Alvin was about people and now. With Graham, if she said stop, you'd FREEZE. God help you if you had an itch. With Ailey, the movement kept flowing even when you stopped. Also, the Ailey company gave me the opportunity to dance the works of many choreographers, allowing me to grow. I learned a lot and I continue to learn a lot."

In the early 60's, touring took Williams to Europe, Australia and Southeast Asia. "It was a fabulous experience; I'd do exactly the same thing if I had it to do all over again. Martha and Alvin taught the London critics about modern dance." In 1960, Ailey choreographed a classic masterpiece of American Modern Dance *Revelations*, a monumental work based on the black religious experience. During that first decade of the Company's existence, he created some twenty new ballets including *Hermit Songs* (1961) and *Reflections in D* (1962). In 1965, he discovered the extraordinarily talented young dancer Judith Jamison, who, along with Williams and other soloists, helped bring the company to international prominence.

In 1966, the Ailey company was invited to dance at the First World Festival of Negro Arts in Senegal; the performance was one of the most moving experiences in the lives of company members. Of all of the performers at the festival they alone represented dance theater rather than the folklore of a particular region. They were received with wild enthusiasm.

It was in 1966 that Williams first danced "I Want To Be Ready" from *Revelations*, a role in which he continues to give ever deepening, committed and moving performances. Speaking of the dance, Williams recounts, "I find new things in *Revelations* every day. It is so perfectly choreographed, you can't mess it up. You can do it with a dead face or you can bring that light to your chest. Just doing the steps puts you in a performing mode, and it just happens. You're a person going to church, not a ballerina or a modern dancer. You dance what you believe in."

"Kelvin [Rotardier] and I used to sit in the dressing room and say 'Can you imagine watching *Revelations* every day. How does Alvin feel while we are dancing?' That helped us to see it from the inside out, different each time; a new approach."

The roles with which Williams has been particularly associated over the years include a duet in *Blues Suite*, Lazarus in *Mary Lou's Mass*, *Hermit Songs*, *Reflections in D* and *Love Songs*. He is full of reminiscences about working on these roles with Ailey: "Alvin would come into my dressing room and ask 'What are you dancing about? Do you know the music? Why don't you point your foot?' He was a wonderful tyrant because we learned. He always made us aware of what character we were dancing, what we were dancing about."

**Figure 7**   Dudley Williams in Ailey's *Love Songs*.

"As a choreographer, Alvin was always loose; he allowed us freedom in our roles. He'd say 'you do this and this for four counts of eight, then improvise in this type of character.' He would give a framework and you would color it in. The counts and the way the music was used were set, but much was left up to the dancers."

"I remember Alvin showing me a wonderful solo; it had all these twiddley things with the fingers. I said 'Alvin, I can't do that.' He said, 'Chicken [his pet name for Williams], make it your own.'"

"After he choreographed something he left it. He didn't want to see it again; he never came back. But, he did change things from dancer to dancer. He used the dancer like an instrument. If you couldn't do a high C, he took it down an octave. He used you for what you had; each dancer had his own version."

"In group works, however, he cleaned the material quite carefully. If you were smart you blended in. If not, he'd take you out. He took me out of *Blues Suite* because I couldn't do the jazz the way he wanted it. Then he made that funny duet for Bill Louther and me at the end. Bill and I were always acting the fools in rehearsal and Alvin would say 'keep that in.' The section was very free and very funny. After Bill left the company, it got set and it wasn't that funny anymore. Finally, Alvin put a woman into the role, and it was never the same."

"In the early days the company was a family. The eight or ten of us ate together, went to a disco together; we were friends. Then two by two, like Noah's Ark, or four by four, we paired off. Nicola Cernovitch did everything – the payroll, the lights, the costumes."

*Revelations*, the company signature piece, was always learned first, starting with the end group section, "I've Been 'Buked". Then, if the dancer had another role, he or she went on learning; otherwise they waited. *Blues Suite* came next." Now it is common for an incoming dancer to learn roles by guest choreographers rather than starting with an Ailey work.

"After the 60's," Williams reports, "Alvin calmed down a little; in the beginning he was a total tyrant." Glancing at a company photograph from the early period, Williams remembered that Ailey had fired six dancers out of that particular group which numbered about ten or twelve. "That was when Alvin was just coming out of his rage. In Paris we had worked every day, and had only one day off in three weeks."

"He mellowed out with age and the dancers changed. In the early days we were technically good but nothing like the dancers these days. We had other sources to dance from, not just technique. Our bodies weren't perfect but we had 'it,' I call it 'it', that special inner performing quality."

"We certainly had many hardships. I remember being in Milan for weeks without performing, living in a brothel, with someone from the company slipping dollar bills under the door from time to time. We did it, but it wasn't fun. We had to stay; Alvin had our airline tickets."

"I remember being stranded in Barcelona, waiting for Rebecca Harkness to come along and feed us. Finally Bob Powell, Takako [Asakawa] and I, followed shortly by Clive Thompson, insisted on getting our tickets back. We went to London and taught for three weeks and got Robin Howard's London School of Contemporary Dance [The Place] started."

Ailey lived simply and was a rough man. His first allegiance was to the company. When he performed in a Broadway show he saved his money and put it back into the company. He sometimes financed a young choreographer from his own pocket.

From the beginning Ailey was dedicated to the idea of a repertory company and the encouragement of choreographers. "Trying to stimulate choreography is what it's all about," said Ailey. "That was my dream." The list of choreographers whom he encouraged by mounting their works is enormously impressive: Donald

**Figure 8**   A photograph of the company on its European tour, 1966. Dancers include back row left to right: Morton Winslow, James Truitte, 3 unidentified dancers, Alvin Ailey, Kelvin Rotardier; front row left to right: Miguel Godreau, Loretta Abbot, Takako Asakawa, 3 unidentified, Consuela Atlas, Judith Jamison.

McKayle, Talley Beatty, Louis Johnson, George Faison, Eleo Pomare, Billy Wilson, Ulysses Dove, Donald Byrd, Bill T. Jones, Pearl Primus, Janet Collins and Judith Jamison.

And, he didn't like the words "black dance." He said, "Good dance is good dance. It's not black or green or purple or white. Dance is just good or it's bad." Thus, these other choreographers whose work he staged: Ted Shawn, May O'Donnell, Rudy Perez, Lar Lubovitch, Hans Van Manen, Choo-San Goh, Glen Tetley, John Butler, Joyce Trisler, Anna Sokolow, Jennifer Muller, Elisa Monte, and Brian MacDonald.

Since its inception, the Alvin Ailey American Dance Theater has performed for an estimated 15,000,000 people in forty-eight states, forty-five countries on six continents, earning a reputation as one of the most popular international ambassadors of American culture. The company's extensive touring schedule has included annual United States tours as well as more than twenty-five international forays highlighted by a trip to the USSR in 1970, the first for an American modern dance company since the days of Isadora Duncan, and by the first modern dance company visit to the People's Republic of China.

Since 1972, the company has appeared annually at New York's City Center Theater and has also performed at the New York State Theater and the Metropolitan Opera House in Lincoln Center. It was featured on several Public Broadcasting System and various other network television specials as well as on both German and Italian television.

**Figure 9**   Dudley Williams teaching company class. In the front row, third from left, Judith Jamison, Michele Murray; second row from left, Kenneth Pearl, Miguel Godreau, Clive Thompson.

Although there were a lot of discouraging times when Ailey almost gave up the company for lack of money, thirty odd years later it is still functioning and growing. And, Ailey loved when the company grew. It was when John Butler's *Carmina Burana* was first staged that Ailey knew that he needed more people. He had a global view, and was always looking for new things, new ideas and growth.

Ailey received many prizes and awards in recognition of his achievements: several honorary doctorate degrees including one from Princeton University; the NAACP Spingarn Medal in 1976; the New York City Mayor's Award of Arts and Culture in 1977; and the United Nations Peace Medal in 1982. He garnered all three of the dance world's major honors: the Dance Magazine Award in 1975; the Capezio Award in 1979; and the Samuel H. Scripps American Dance Festival Award in 1987.

In 1988, Ailey received the much coveted Kennedy Center Honor for his extraordinary contribution to American culture and achievement in the performing arts, just in time. He didn't look well, but his company members who saw him every day didn't notice.

He never let up on his driven pace. He was supposed to join the company for its 1989 European tour, but in each city his appearance was postponed. Finally, in Copenhagen, the company was informed that he was dying. Williams flew back to the United States and saw him the day before his last.

"Hi Chicken, you're here," was what he heard. "We were good friends, Alvin and I. I am so happy that I had the chance to tell him I love him, and to thank him for the opportunity he gave me to dance on his stage."

Yes, Ailey had a global vision. His last act was to conceive of the headquarters at 211 West Sixty-first Street, a full floor of the building, with four studios, a staff of over fifty people, a booming school with over three thousand students in one hundred thirty classes weekly, an enormous outreach program, several dance

**Figure 10**  Ailey teaching in Brazil, 1978.

camps for children at risk, and two performing companies. Although he conceived of the headquarters, he did not live to see it actually peopled with students and staff.

With the move to the Sixty-first street building, one of Ailey's dreams belatedly came true. I asked Williams how Ailey felt about all of this growth and grandiosity. Williams replied that Ailey always got bored with what he had. " Had he lived, he probably would have wanted a whole building with a theater or perhaps even more."

After Ailey's death, Judith Jamison was appointed company director. In a tribute to her mentor, she said:

Alvin Ailey radiated life. And dance was the prism through which he made visible the spectrum of our experiences. He was a lamp around which dancers gathered and often held aloft for guidance . . . His radiant spirit lives on in the company he poured his very soul into; our extended limbs an extension of his body which, though grand and eloquent, was never big enough to contain his expansive spirit.

THE ALVIN AILEY AMERICAN DANCE THEATRE

**Figure 11**    The Company.

*Choreography and Dance*, 1996, Vol 4(1), pp. 21–27
Photocopying permitted by license only

# Alvin Ailey and the Alvin Ailey American Dance Center

Denise Jefferson

In 1969, Alvin Ailey founded his school, the American Dance Center, in Brooklyn, New York, and moved it to Manhattan in 1970. Through his vision and philosophy of dance training, it has grown from 125 to its current size of over 3,000 students, creating a true dance center and an egalitarian community of young artists of diverse races and ethnic backgrounds. Ailey's involvement with all aspects of the school and his sensitive and inspirational leadership are the subjects of the story of the American Dance Center.

KEY WORDS   Lester Horton, Katherine Dunham, Judith Jamison

It seems appropriate to start with a description of the American Dance Center and a little of its history before beginning my personal memoir.

## The Structure

In 1969, Alvin Ailey founded the Alvin Ailey American Dance Center in Brooklyn, New York, with an initial enrollment of 125 students. In 1970, Ailey joined forces with Pearl Lang to establish the American Dance Center in Manhattan. Today, under my direction, a prestigious faculty trains approximately 3,000 students annually, offering more than 130 classes weekly. Located in New York City's Lincoln Center area, the American Dance Center houses four spacious studios, student and faculty lounges, dressing rooms, a library, a dance wear boutique and administrative offices. Students are drawn from every part of the world representing a diversity of racial and ethnic backgrounds. The Dance Center offers a comprehensive curriculum including Horton technique, ballet, Dunham technique (Afro-Caribbean), Graham-based modlern dance, jazz and tap. The school curriculum also includes classes in barre à terre, body conditioning, yoga, repertory, Techniques of Performance, dance composition, dance history, improvisation, music, theater arts and voice. Guided by the belief that dance instruction should be made available to everyone, the Center has designed a number of programs which offer professional training at all levels. The school is divided into two divisions according to the age of the students: the Junior division for ages 3 to 15, and the Professional division for ages 15 and older. The Junior Division offers several programs from creative dance for younger students to the Pre-Professional program with a six-level graded curriculum, with a diversity of dance techniques mirroring that of the Professional Division. In the Professional division a variety of programs are offered:

The Alvin Ailey Fellowship Program is designed for students ages 16 to 21 who are at an intermediate level in ballet and modern dance and who exhibit the highest potential for a performing career. It is a full-time, two year training program for which students are chosen by audition. There is also the possibility of partial scholarship study for high school students, who attend the Dance Center part-time during the academic year and full time in the summer.

The Certificate Program is a full-time training program for high school graduates age 17 to 23 who wish to pursue a professional career in the dance field and have achieved at least an advanced beginner level in both ballet and modern dance. The two year curriculum is based on a conservatory model which combines in-depth technical training and performance experience with dance academics and creative courses. Admission to the program is by audition.

Other programs offered by the Center include an Independent Study Program for students from the United States and from abroad, a Summer Intensive and an intensive winter session called the January Experience. All levels of technique classes, from elementary to professional, are also open to the general public.

The American Dance Center serves as the official school of the Alvin Ailey American Dance Theater, for which it maintains rehearsal facilities. A junior company, the Alvin Ailey Repertory Ensemble, is the resident company of the school. The Alvin Ailey American Dance Center, the Alvin Ailey American Dance Theater and the Alvin Ailey Repertory Ensemble operate under the auspices of Dance Theater Foundation, Inc.

**Figure 12**   A class at the Alvin Ailey American Dance Center. Photo copyright Beatriz Schiller.

## Remembering Alvin

In 1969, Alvin Ailey faced a crossroads. He was forced to relocate his company, the Alvin Ailey American Dance Theater, and his school of 125 students from Brooklyn. Pearl Lang, longtime soloist with the Martha Graham Company, had found a three story church at 229 East Fifty-ninth Street in Manhattan, into which she had settled her dance company. She needed a compatible artistic partner with whom to share the rent and she had heard about Alvin's dilemma. The two talked and realized that, although they had come from two distinctly different traditions in the American modern dance world, Horton and Graham, they had similar needs. They both had to have space for their companies and both wanted to establish a school. The American Dancer Center was founded in 1970 by these two artists. Before, between and after rehearsals, their company members taught the techniques of Graham, Horton, classical ballet, and jazz. They were the first American Dance Center faculty.

The top floor, studio C, became the ballet studio; the middle floor, studio B was the rehearsal studio for Ailey's company and housed the larger classes in Horton, jazz and Graham techniques. Studio A, on the ground floor, was used for rehearsals of the Pearl Lang Dance Company and the smaller technique classes. The combined energy of the two companies in residence and the variety of technical classes, all with wonderful live accompaniment, created a high energy that was sensed the minute one entered the fire engine red door.

Ailey wanted a school with a curriculum diverse enough to train dancers for his company. For him, the perfect dancer had "a ballet bottom (gorgeous feet and legs) and a modern dance top (a supple, expressive torso)." He wanted dancers who were trained to be equally proficient in classical ballet, the modern dance techniques of Lester Horton, Martha Graham and Katherine Dunham, and jazz. He wanted dancers who were actors, dancers who understood that to dance was to communicate intimately with the audience. Dancing was to be a vibrant, living act that would transcend the traditional barriers of race, language and economics. He did not want his school to be an elitist institution; he wished to make dance accessible to everybody. He wanted a "dance center", an artistic community that, in addition to training dance artists, would be a laboratory for emerging choreographers and would sponsor a host of events from art exhibits, to seminars, to dance concerts.

Alvin Ailey was a man with a large, embracing spirit. His enthusiasm for what was innovative, unusual and daring, and his ability rapidly to sketch, from thin air, the most exciting ideas for new projects made him an almost quicksilver energy force. He wanted the school to be filled with students of all races, from very diverse backgrounds. In 1973, when the American Dance Center received its first grant from the New York State Council for the Arts, which helped establish the first professional training program called the Scholarship Program, Alvin wanted audition advertisements to be placed in foreign language newspapers as well as in the African-American press so that a truly international community of students would have the opportunity to study dance. There were approximately 150 scholarship recipients in that first year, including Sarita Allen who, the following year, became a charter member of the school's resident company, the Alvin Ailey Repertory Ensemble.

Alvin loved the studio: the space, the work, the possibilities for creativity. But, most of all, he loved his dancers. One day, as I entered the American Dance Center to rehearse with Pearl Lang, Alvin took my arm and insisted that I join a group of dancers, students, teachers and musicians, in an alcove under the stairs, in order to view rough cuts of *Memories and Visions*, a television special about him and his company. He focused completely on the dancers, speeding fast forward through those sections about him personally and those he narrated, to play again and again the sections which pleased him most, the ones with the dancers. He told us to look for this exquisite moment and that divine position. The technique and artistry of a dancer was what truly captured him. I loved hearing him wonder at those transcendent moments in which his dancers were caught by the camera lens.

Alvin liked to make unannounced, surprise visits in the school. He had a touching respect for what he viewed as the almost sacred contract between the teacher, accompanist and the student in the studio. Rarely would he enter a studio to observe class unless it was being taught by one of a handful of faculty members with whom he had historical ties. Among these few were Nat Horne, Walter Raines and Joan Peters. He would, however, ask me or other staff members for the video monitor and certain tapes. He would assemble students, parents, faculty and musicians in the Student Lounge or any other open space, to see the videos. He would talk to the students about their dreams, goals and ambitions, giving them priceless advice and recounting anecdotes before vanishing into his upstairs office.

Alvin had an eye that could pierce the external structure of a dance student and see the gifts within. Perhaps because he, himself, started formal dance training relatively late, at age nineteen or twenty, and had an athlete's muscular body, he was particularly supportive of the older male students. A number of them found their way into his office, and he encouraged them to continue to pursue their dreams. He also believed in nurturing emerging choreographers and filled his company's repertoire with the early works of Ulysses Dove, Elisa Monte, George Faison and Donald Byrd. The daring and trailblazing energy of their dances renewed him and made a perfect balance with the more classical works of his colleagues Talley Beatty, Donald McKayle and John Butler.

In 1984, when he appointed me director of his school, the Alvin Ailey American Dance Center, he gave me several gifts; the greatest of them was his faith in my ability to do this almost overwhelming job. It was my great fortune to have had five years of working with him in this capacity and to have had annual planning sessions with him each summer. He gave me the space to experiment, to discover what worked and what didn't, without making me feel that I was in a judgmental fish bowl. When I discussed my plans with him, he would say, "Really? What will you want to do now?" He always encouraged me to have bigger dreams, to err through generosity rather than caution.

Alvin believed in training the whole dancer: the body, the mind and the spirit. He read voraciously, collected art and listened to music of all kinds. In 1981, the school formed a committee headed by Sylvia Waters, Artistic Director of the Alvin Ailey Repertory Ensemble, Jeanne Noble, education consultant, and me, to expand its curriculum in preparation for its initial accreditation application. He was very pleased that courses in Dance History, Music, Theater Arts, Improvisation, and Dance Composition were added. He often cited as the model his years at the Lester Horton School, where students choreographed, designed and executed costumes and scenery, studied Dance History and Music, and regularly went to art exhibits. As the students in the school became better technicians, Alvin began to involve himself more in their training. In the mid-1980's, the school had an unusually talented group of male high school students from the La Guardia High School of Performing Arts. Walter Raines was director of the Scholarship Program and chairperson of our ballet department. Walter and I decided that he would teach a special boys class twice weekly to supplement their fine training in Graham-based modern dance, Horton technique and jazz. Alvin and Walter had long talks about methods to develop that ideal dancer with the "ballet bottom and the modern top." What resulted from those talks and the work in the class was stunning. From the class came many dancers who went on to major careers with world renown companies: Troy Powell with the Alvin Ailey Repertory Ensemble and the Alvin Ailey American Dance Theater; Desmond Richardson, with the Alvin Ailey Repertory Ensemble, the Alvin Ailey American Dance Theater and currently the Frankfurt Ballet; Jean Emile with the Netherlands Dance Theater, Compania Naciónal de Danza and currently the Lar Lubovich Dance Company; Sant'gria Bello with the New York City Ballet and Charles Ferrugio with the Pacific Northwest Ballet.

In 1986, Alvin involved himself even more actively in the professional training of students in the school. Two years before, to the delight of all of us, Judith Jamison had created her first ballet, *Divining*, with the advanced students. She gave them much insight about performing, about taking incredible risks –'' going to the wall'' – in the workshop. She shared her spirit as much as her choreography, a legacy from her years of working with Alvin and on Broadway. Alvin was so impressed with the process that he decided that he, himself, would give a workshop for the advanced students. He used the workshop to develop movement material for his new ballet *Caverna Magica*.

On the first day, he sat all of the students in a circle and asked them to talk about their dreams and their career goals. He asked probing and challenging questions, forcing them to delve inside for answers while giving supportive guidance. The next day the students started to move, with Alvin pushing them to be physically daring and to reveal their more vulnerable sides.

This experience was so beneficial that he and I made arrangements to offer the same "laboratory" situation to Talley Beatty the following year. Beatty reconstructed *Come and Get The Beauty Of It Hot* with our advanced students in the spring of 1987 before mounting it with the Alvin Ailey American Dance Theater the following summer.

In his last years with us, Alvin focused for the first time on the children in our Junior Division. Perhaps he saw them as the next generation and wanted to inspire them with certain ideas and feelings. He would drop in the school on Saturday late mornings, sit in the reception area and talk with the children or show videos of his company. Some of the more daring ones would sit on his lap and sell him raffle tickets. One Saturday stands out in my memory as a powerful example of his brilliance and inclusiveness. The Parents' Association wished to give him a plaque, and he arrived, somewhat late, for the children's June presentation. The first two groups of the younger students had already performed their group dance. Alvin walked center stage and took the microphone. He started to describe to the parents what a challenge dance classes were for their children, bringing onto the floor to demonstrate various young ones whom he had chosen extemporaneously. Then he asked parent volunteers to join them executing these steps. The children loved it because, of course, they were the experts and their parents the novices. He next asked for testimonials from parents concerning why they brought their children to the American Dance Center to study dance. The responses were moving, sincere and totally spontaneous. Alvin had shifted the whole focus of the performance from a formal presentation to a happening with parents, children and teacher moving and speaking together. It was truly a familial experience and one we treasure forever. He had the courage always to follow his instincts. They never failed him; he was truly a man of the theater.

**Figure 13**   The children. Photo copyright Marbeth, 1992.

In looking back at my years with Alvin and at his legacy for all of us, one thing keeps recurring. Alvin always believed that one's dream should be the driving force in one's life and that ways to realize it would appear if one kept that dream vibrant in one's head and heart.

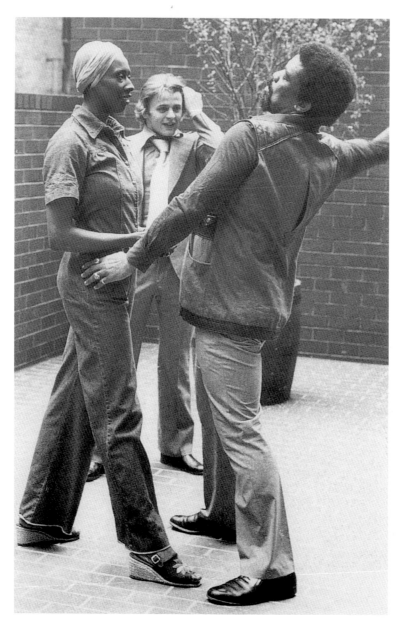

**Figure 14**  Ailey with Judith Jamison and Mikhail Baryshnikov, 1976. Photo copyright Jack Vartoogian.

Choreography and Dance, 1996, Vol 4(1), pp. 29–34
Photocopying permitted by license only

# Alvin Ailey Repertory Ensemble

Sylvia Waters

The Alvin Ailey Repertory Ensemble is one of the most promising components of the American Dance Center, the official school of the Alvin Ailey American Dance Theater. The Repertory Ensemble was established in the fall of 1974. Since its inception, it has been very successful in serving its dual functions as both an arena for performance exposure for twelve promising students and a vehicle through which new audiences throughout the country can be exposed to dance.

KEY WORDS    Judith Jamison, Bicentennial Celebration, Duke Ellington

Alvin Ailey's devotion to the development of young artists, combined with his interest in expanding and educating dance audiences, prompted the establishment of the Alvin Ailey Repertory Ensemble. In the fall of 1974 Alvin formed a workshop comprised of the most outstanding scholarship students of the American Dance Center. This hand-picked group of dancers became the original members of the Alvin Ailey Repertory Ensemble.

At the outset, the formation of what was then called the Alvin Ailey Repertory Workshop, under the direction of Karina Riegger, was a way for Alvin to have both time and the availability of twelve very gifted dancers with whom to work out new choreography. The touring schedule of the Alvin Ailey American Dance Theater was so rigorous that rehearsal time to do new works was woefully inadequate. This made it increasingly difficult for him to feel that any new work created under these circumstances was truly crystallized.

Utilizing dancers from the scholarship program to prepare the Ellington tribute for the United States Bicentennial Celebration seemed the ideal solution. It was this group of young artists that appeared in the CBS television special "Ailey Celebrates Ellington" in the fall of 1974. In turn these works were transferred to the Alvin Ailey American Dance Theater and presented at the New York State Theater in New York City for the Bicentennial Celebration in 1976. Shortly after its inception, Alvin asked me to become artistic director of the Ensemble, a post I have held and enjoyed ever since.

The Ensemble, which evolved into the Company-in-Residence of the Alvin Ailey American Dance Center, provides young artists with technical training, coaching and first hand experience working with emerging as well as seasoned choreographers whose reputations have been long established. Extensive performance opportunities offer an invaluable link between training and the profession, a link which is not available to many young artists who wish to make their careers in dance.

It was not unusual and always rewarding when Alvin made time in his full schedule to rehearse his ballets. He kept a keen eye on the up and coming choreographic talent and the developing performers. The atmosphere was supercharged by his presence. He generously provided images that inspired the dancers. He enriched them with information that created a deeper understanding

**Figure 15**   The Alvin Ailey Repertory Ensemble in Donald McKayle's *Games*, 1976. Singers in window are Mary Barnett, who restaged the work, and Alister Butler; dancers, from left, are Dianne Macong, Clayton Palmer, Ronni Favors, Steve Mones, Ellis Frazier, Marla Bingham. Photo copyright Rosemary Winckley.

of a movement, a phrase of music or the dancer him or herself, warmly encouraging each one to fully investigate the material, to be more self-demanding, to take chances.

At times Alvin would "individualize" a movement from one of his most classic works (such as "Sinner Man" or "I Want to be Ready" from *Revelations*), further challenging the abilities and still untapped strengths of the Ensemble, helping each dancer to make the transition from technician to performer to artist.

His accessibility to the dancers in the Repertory Ensemble was exciting, and typical. It remains a privilege to dance these expressive, dynamic masterworks, to be challenged by and connected to the source of one's inspiration. These moments with Alvin were treasured as they raised the standards of the dancer's personal expectations.

Alvin was artistic advisor to the Repertory Ensemble; his council and encouragement was most inspiring and a formidable lesson in human relations as well as in theater. The sharing of energy, vision and dreams was truly a gift which helped me shape the Repertory Ensemble's mission, aesthetic, and the quality of it's presentations.

Judith Jamison, a longtime colleague, and Ailey's successor, is just as energetic a supporter of the Repertory Ensemble. Her artistry and enthusiasm bring the necessary continuity to this very vital component of the Ailey organization.

**Figure 16** One audience member's impression of *Revelations*, sent to Sylvia Waters, Artistic Director of the Alvin Ailey Repertory Ensemble.

Membership in the Ensemble is by invitation. The twelve members are chosen on the basis of my monitoring of advanced level classes, auditions, studio performances in the school, as well as consultation with the faculty and Denise Jefferson, the school director. In order to ensure their growth, the dancers receive ongoing evaluation of individual strengths and weaknesses in the studio and in more formal conferences with me. In addition, on occasion, Judith Jamison and Masazumi Chaya, Associate Artistic Director of the Alvin Ailey American Dance Theater, personally observe, direct and coach the dancers offering them invaluable insights on their work and on the dances. Repertory Ensemble members may remain in the Company for two, or occasionally three years, after which many go on either to the Alvin Ailey American Dance Theater or to other professional companies, most recently the Garth Fagan Company, Ballet Hispanico, Dayton Contemporary Dance Company, the Donald Byrd Company, Shapiro and Smith and Elise Monte. Many "graduates" have appeared on the commercial stage, in television and film.

The dancers receive a weekly stipend for 40 weeks as well as a per diem when touring. Thirty weeks of performing are preceded by a ten week rehearsal period during which the young artists work with both established and emerging choreographers in the creation of new works and the restaging of existing ballets. During the 1993–94 season the repertory consisted of five of Ailey's dances including his challenging early ballet *Blues Suite*, his *Reflections in D* to a score by Duke Ellington, as well as his masterpiece *Revelations*. Also in the repertory were dances choreographed by Kevin Jeff, Eleo Pomare, Daniel Shapiro and Joanie Smith, and Kevin Wynn. Previous seasons have included choreography by Talley Beatty, Ulysses Dove, Ralph Lemon and Warren Spears, and Judith Jamison, prior to her assuming her current position as artistic director of the Alvin Ailey American Dance Theater and artistic advisor to the Repertory Ensemble.

New dance audiences are developed through the Repertory Ensemble's wide range of performance sites in atraditional settings such as community and senior citizen centers, universities, and rehabilitation facilities. The company performs for over 40,000 people annually, including those whose opportunity to see professional dance is severely limited. In the 1994–95 season, the Ensemble performed in 35 cities in 17 states. Such touring addresses a critical need by providing professional dance and educational activities at an affordable cost.

The performing experience includes: full concerts in national tours to smaller theaters and communities, most often in university settings, throughout the United States and the Caribbean; an annual season at Aaron Davis Hall in New York City; an Arts in Education Outreach component which consists of lecture/demonstrations, master classes and informal discussions for students from kindergarten through college. It is those dancers who show an aptitude for teaching who give the master classes allowing them an additional experience to prepare them for the "real world." Additionally, the one-on-one informal discussions give the dancers the opportunity to be role models, adding to their communication and teaching skills, while providing a positive experience for the youngsters with whom they meet.

Through these extensive performance opportunities, the dancers are able to expand their view of the world as well as improve their performance technique and stamina. When they emerge from the Repertory Ensemble, they are seasoned performers.

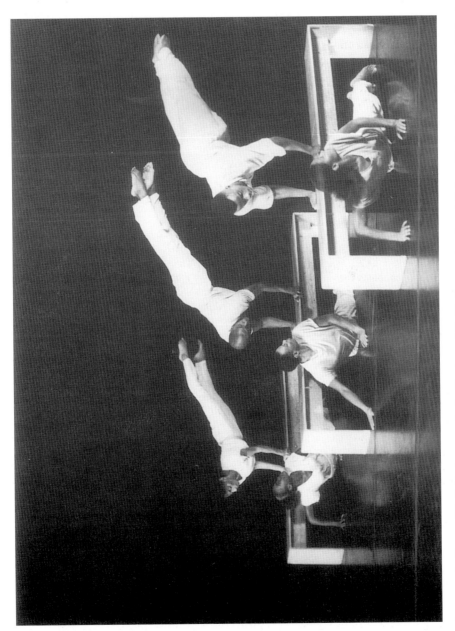

**Figure 17** *To Have and To Hold*, choreography by Shapiro and Smith. Dancers: top, from left: Lana Gordon, Jason Reynolds, Michael Bennett; bottom: Solange Sandy, Torens Johnson, Yvette Perry. Photo copyright Beatriz Schiller.

Since its inception, the Ensemble has won critical acclaim. Writing of the April 1992, sold-out performances during its New York season at Aaron Davis Hall at City College, Jennifer Dunning of *The New York Times* said, "By now the vibrancy and accomplished dancing of the Alvin Ailey Repertory Ensemble should come as no surprise. But the group outdid itself . . . in a performance that stood out for its artistry and sophistication."

**Figure 18**   Solange Sandy and Derrick Minter in Kevin Jeff's *Seeds*. Photo copyright Beatriz Schiller.

*Choreography and Dance*, 1996, Vol 4(1), pp. 35–40
Photocopying permitted by license only

# Life With Alvin: A Kansas City Story

Allan S. Gray II

*Life With Alvin* gives an image of what it was like to share a multi-faceted friendship with Alvin Ailey. It tells of his involvement in Kansas City, where he was much more than a choreographer or dancer. He was part of the humanity of the community, a community with which he shared his dreams and which helped transform them into reality. These reflections are written to illustrate the humanitarian side of this great artist.

KEY WORDS   Kansas City; The Kansas City Friends of Alvin Ailey; Harry Belafonte; Charlie Parker; jazz

**Figure 19**   Author Allan Gray with Alvin Ailey.

In the fall of 1982, I stood, unsuspecting, in the corridor of the airport in Kansas City. The wooden archways of the ceiling gave way to the gently sweeping corridor of the terminal. From around the passageway, an endless stream of humanity destined for places unknown weaved its way colorfully into and out of view around the terminal's curved walls. The sounds, sights and smells of modern day travel sparred for the attention of my senses.

35

Like the anxious throngs around me, I checked the arrival monitor, as I had only moments before. The flight was still on time, an anomaly in this age of deregulation. My gaze remained fixed on the gate as one by one passengers began to exit from the aircraft.

"What does he look like?" I asked a companion equally as intent and uncertain as I. The sounds of the airport were much louder now, as passenger after passenger slowly emerged from the canyon of plate glass and united with friends, business acquaintances, limousine drivers and crying children long past their patience thresholds.

Suddenly an unforgettable image of a man moved stealth-like down the narrow passageway. That must be the one. I remember thinking, like most who saw him in his later years, "He doesn't look much like a dancer." Streaks of white peeked from behind the strands of the black hair of his beard in a zebra-like pattern. The colors of his beard belied his age. The eyes gazed distantly, as if seeing into another cosmos beyond the sudden excitement surrounding his arrival. They were dark, yet friendly and full of life. These were not ordinary eyes. These were eyes that had witnessed much of the world. They had gazed upon kings and a river of humanity in all manner of costume and posture. They had basked in the beauty of a sunset over China; they had seen a million people rise in triumphant applause.

In the years that passed, I often reflected on that day and thought: If I had only known then that from that meeting forward, my life would be forever changed, I might have been even more nervous. If, at that moment, I had had a full appreciation of the man, his genius, his place in the world and its history, I might have reveled more in our meeting.

Without ceremony and with a calming sense of humility came the words, "Hi, I'm Alvin Ailey. And you must be Allan?" In that moment, I was overcome by an intimate, almost spiritual, feeling of human connection. Alvin's warmth was disarming. I felt as if I had just welcomed an old friend back home from a long journey, not that I had met one of the great choreographers of our time. This meeting was the beginning of a once in a lifetime friendship and the beginning, as well, of a new era of Alvin's life.

In my reflections on life with Alvin, it is difficult to assimilate adequately all the pieces into any coherent structure. Our conversations would take flight on wings of thoughts, ideas, philosophies, emotions, dreams. I would often call Alvin, for no particular reason, just to see if all was well, only to find him in a state of mind in which he needed to confide or talk through a situation. Most often I would simply listen. But there were times when my counsel was sought and, to my amazement, acted upon.

One of my fondest memories is of one night while I was in New York. I received a call from Alvin inviting me to dinner with some friends. It was only during the cab ride that I discovered that the friends were Harry and Julie Belafonte, and that dinner was to be at their condo on the west side of Manhattan!

Another memory: As a twenty-nine year old man strolling with Alvin through the historic streets of 18th and Vine in Kansas City, I was moved by Alvin's understanding of the struggles of African Americans and the relationship of art and music to our lives. Alvin came to 18th and Vine in silent tribute to the ghosts of the jazz legends that had been a foundation of his musical make-up. Alvin had a special relationship with all music, but particularly with jazz. It was jazz that gave him the vocabulary to describe the unique experiences of African Americans.

Arguably, if gospel music was the spirit of Alvin's musical expression, jazz was the heart. Its rhythm bred life into every work he created.

The more we discussed Kansas City jazz, the more animated Alvin became, as if a thousand ideas were bursting for release to be born again and, through dance, tell their stories. He spoke about Duke Ellington, Count Basie, Ella Fitzgerald, Mary Lou Williams, Billie Holiday, Jay McShann and the unforgettable Charlie "Bird" Parker.

Alvin was particularly interested in Charlie Parker and his influences on the development of jazz and music as we know it. It was during this first visit that we initially discussed Alvin's dream of paying tribute and homage to one of Kansas City's jazz hero's, Charlie "Yardbird" Parker. In addition to having a certain fascination with Charlie Parker the artist, Alvin had a very private, deeply felt personal connection. In some vague manner, Alvin seemed to relate to Parker and the tragedy of his life as if part of Parker's story were his own.

Alvin not only wanted to create a lasting dance tribute to Parker, but also to use the work to inspire a community he had grown to love. I remember the warm autumn afternoon when Alvin first shared these ideas with me. I recall literally sitting on the edge of my seat riding with Alvin in a limousine to get his hair cut. We meandered through the heart of the ghetto to the only barber shop with which I was familiar. As I shared with him the history of our community and gave him accounts of my childhood memories of each corner that passed, Alvin began to reflect on his personal views of community and our responsibility for our fellow man.

He spoke of how disheartened he was to realize that with each passing generation we separate ourselves from our own people through class, economic, educational and social positioning. He noted how the arts were, in his vision of humanity, one of the constants available to re-unite us with ourselves.

Alvin painted a picture of a community linked by dance. For the first time, I began to see clearly how the arts, once an inseparable part of the richness of our lives, had been severed from the very people who most understood and appreciated their true values and meanings. I realized what a powerful force art was in our lives and how very necessary it was to the security of our existence as a people. It was as if Alvin, who was so inspired by Lester Horton, wanted to expand upon the gift his own mentor had given him.

To Alvin, art and dance were not mere niceties reserved for those who could afford the price of admission to the theater. Nor were they meant to be guarded from the people behind the granite walls of museums. Art and all its disciplines were a life force to be celebrated, valued, embraced, and worn like a cloak by all people regardless of their particular backgrounds. The art of dance is part of the human experience we all share. It was this commonality of experiences in art that enable us to strip ourselves of the barriers that separate us, and through its power, renew our faith in one another, and see our communities, our friends, our families, and ourselves with new eyes not jaundiced by prejudice. Alvin saw his mission as taking dance out of staid performance halls and sharing it with the very people who needed it most. In his vision, the arts have almost medicinal influences on the ills of society.

I remember Alvin saying that of all the things he had accomplished as a choreographer and artistic director, what gave him the most satisfaction was bringing his dance to the people, especially the children. What I soon realized was

**Figure 20**   Ailey with Coretta Scott King. Photo by Jack Vartoogian.

that this was not merely a chance conversation, but Alvin was entrusting me with his life's vision. I became totally inspired by his way of thinking, and soon had a new mission of my own – to help make Alvin's dream come alive.

Over the next seven years, Alvin weaved a glorious tapestry of his vision in countless conversations, which we jokingly called our fantasy sessions. They were totally unplanned, always over a meal. We would discuss our ideas for the company and Kansas City. We would plan every detail and then Alvin, with a heavy sigh, would lean back, raise his hands in mock surrender, and say, "O.K., now what can we really do? I don't know how to make all these pieces fit. You know?" He proceeded to draw upon his vast wealth of experience and people, and fit each individual into his or her appropriate place: Donny McKayle, Bill T. Jones, Talley Beatty, Todd Bolender to create new works; Gary Deloatch to teach dance at a school for disadvantaged students; Chaya to maintain the company's spirit and balance for a long tour; Carol Garner to bring *Caverna Magica* visually alive; Ulysses Dove, Garth Fagan, Pearl Primus and Katherine Dunham to illustrate some of the greatest choreography of our century.

To make Alvin's vision a reality, I established an organization that was to become known as the Kansas City Friends of Alvin Ailey (KCFAA). We became the second home for the Alvin Ailey American Dance Theater, and the mechanism that brought substance to the dream. It was a vehicle that gave a new sense of purpose to the lives of thousands of people in Kansas City and around the world.

KCFAA became the prototype for demonstrating how to unite communities and embrace new paradigms of diversity. In this new vision, cultures and people are valued and celebrated in new ways through the experience of dance.

It was in Kansas City that Alvin was provided with new, fertile ground to create and dream. In this nurturing environment, outside the tug and pulls of New York, Alvin was given the chance to work in a community that asked only how it could share in making his vision a reality. Here the seeds of Alvin's vision blossomed in ways he had not allowed even himself to dream. New works were created including: *For Bird With Love, Caverna Magica,* and *Opus McShann*; a major and historic community arts in education program that spanned the borders of Missouri and Kansas was initiated; AileyCamp, a nationally replicated summer dance camp for children at risk, was founded; unprecedented, sold out performances took place; and there evolved a coming together of people of all races, religions, and ethnicities centered around the dance.

What always amazed me about Alvin was his ability to make everyone around him feel he or she had a personal relationship with him. No matter how many receptions, galas or meetings we would attend together, I would invariably find Alvin camped out in some obscure part of the room talking quietly with a "nobody". This happened in spite of his legendary protest against attending these events. I can still remember him wailing over yet another "three minutes of comments". I never understood this, given that he was such an eloquent speaker, always speaking without notes and able to hold forth on an infinite number of subjects. It was only shortly before his passing that he finally shared with me that he suffered from a deep fear of public speaking. This was who Alvin was: quiet, dignified, eloquent, educated, traveled, regal, yet so very, very private, so very, very human.

I still feel Alvin's spirit on warm autumn days and reflect upon our times together. Each season, when the Alvin Ailey American Dance Theater performs in Kansas City, I still expect to see him at the back row of the theater right before curtain whispering his notes, absorbing all to be seen through those remarkable eyes. Alvin will always be alive and with us as long as there are children inspired to dance and a community with courage to allow love to triumph over hatred, joy to reign over despair and hope to fill our lives and release our inner spirits to dance.

**Figure 21**   Ailey and the company with Bishop Desmond Tutu in the mid 1980s.

*Choreography and Dance*, 1996, Vol 4(1), pp. 41–46
Photocopying permitted by license only

# AileyCamp

Ronnie Favors

AileyCamp is an unique summer day camp program designed to help underserved children ages eleven to thirteen discover their own self-worth. It is not the mission of AileyCamp to train these children to be professional dancers but rather to challenge them to excel through "the four A's – Acceptance, Attention, Appreciation and Affection." The six week project, which is provided free of charge to the youngsters and their families, began in 1989 under the aegis of the Kansas City Friends of Alvin Ailey, an incredible group of volunteers. Thanks to their vision and hard work, the AileyCamp program is now benefiting young people in Kansas City, New York, Baltimore and Frostburg, Maryland.

KEY WORDS   Kansas City Friends of Alvin Ailey; Children's Aid Society; Frostburg; at risk; self-esteem; role models

**Figure 22**  Jeffrey Ferguson leading a jazz class at CAS/AileyCamp, summer 1991. Photo by Bill Schropp.

AileyCamp is a summer program which uses dance as a vehicle for developing self-esteem, creative expression and critical thinking skills among middle school students (ages 11 to 13) at risk of dropping out of school. Several years ago we asked a pioneering group of young people to imagine what it would be like to go to camp and dance all day! They not only imagined what it would be like, they made it a reality. Because of their hard work and dedication to the idea that dance can be fun and good for you too, the AileyCamp project is thriving and expanding into a nationwide program.

The idea for a summer camp where dance is the focus began some years ago as a dream among members of the Kansas City Friends of Alvin Ailey, a volunteer group who make it possible for the world renowned Ailey Company to perform in Kansas City each year. Alvin Ailey, founder and artistic director of the Alvin Ailey American Dance Theater, knew what it was like to spend a summer in the hot city with little to do. He understood how dancing could make a summer day spin into action, taking with it a stage full of energetic youngsters to destinations yet unimagined. Ailey really cared not only about dance, but about the next generation.

How would they succeed if there were not helping hands? Determined to be one of those helping hands, Ailey and Denise Jefferson, director of his school, the Alvin Ailey American Dance Center, worked with the Kansas City Friends. After several years of dreaming, and many months of planning, AileyCamp began its first season in June, 1989, in Kansas City.

**Figure 23**   AileyCamp, Kansas City, 1990.

Who could predict that four weeks of AileyCamp could transform children, so out of shape that they could not complete five minutes of physical activity, into motivated dynamos enduring hours of rehearsals? Who could foresee that a student so lacking in math skills that he could not translate spatial relationships into five equal steps could choreograph a complete, original dance sequence while movingly reciting a poem? Who could imagine that students who were reluctant to stand and give their names on the first day would clamor to perform four weeks later? Who could anticipate that one-fourth of AileyCampers would feel so connected to the people and the experience that KCFAA would be compelled to activate an emergency youth services network to find ongoing post-camp activities?

The impact of AileyCamp was so great that Ailey, already in declining health, travelled to Kansas City in order to see the end-of-camp performance. Expecting to see a regular "kiddie recital," Alvin was amazed to see the AileyCampers performing with confidence and style. In what was to be one of his last public appearances, Alvin conducted a dialogue with the campers, with topics ranging from dance, choreography, and art, to music and sports. It was a moving experience: knowing that Alvin was extremely ill, yet watching him pour his entire energy into exchanging ideas with the newest members of the Ailey family.

The next step in realizing the full potential of AileyCamp was to replicate the program outside Kansas City. By joining forces with the Children's Aid Society which serves more that 100,000 New York families, Dance Theater Foundation was able to open CAS/AileyCamp in the summer of 1991. A two week mini-camp pilot program was also instituted in Baltimore that same year by the Alvin Ailey Dance Theater Foundation of Maryland, followed by the regular AileyCamp program in subsequent summers. AileyCamp/Maryland was such a success in Baltimore that in 1994, another two week pilot program was established in western Maryland, on the campus of Frostburg State University. Planning is now in progress for the opening of AileyCamp in several cities including St. Louis and Philadelphia.

The camp is provided free of charge to the youngsters and their families, and includes all necessities: camp uniforms, leotards and tights, ballet and tap shoes, meals and transportation. The basic AileyCamp structure calls for a six week camp session, five days a week with an enrollment of sixty-five to one hundred children. The Monday through Thursday class schedule includes two daily dance technique classes alternating between ballet, modern dance, jazz and tap; a writing class, and a personal development class. Fridays are special activity days featuring field trips to recreational facilities and cultural institutions. Campers also produce an anthology of their own writings, and star in an end-of-camp performance for family and friends.

AileyCamp is based on the idea that young people do not need many rules in order to have a good time and learn something. AileyCampers are old enough to understand that there are certain basic modes of behavior that ensure a pleasant, safe environment for everyone. Short contracts are signed to help each camper internalize his/her decision to participate in the program. Campers are challenged to excel through "the four A's" as conceived by Debra Leigh, 1989 AileyCamp Project Director: Acceptance, Attention, Appreciation, and Affection.

Classes are small with approximately fifteen to seventeen students in each. AileyCamp dance teachers are "stars" from the Alvin Ailey American Dance Center, positive role models for success in life as well as accomplished masters at translating the discipline of dance into hands-on activities to enhance personal, interpersonal and cognitive skills. Other faculty members in charge of creative writing, theater and personal development are also accomplished professionals. All AileyCamp teachers participate in activities outside their own classrooms, sharing personal experiences during self-esteem classes, assisting with the production of the camp anthology and preparing for the final performance.

**Figure 24**   Michelle De La Uz leading a class on wellness and self-esteem at the CAS/AileyCamp, summer 1991. Photo by Bill Schropp.

Youngsters entering the seventh or eighth grade in the coming school year are eligible to become AileyCampers; they are chosen through a rigorous recruitment process. In Kansas City and Baltimore, recruitment is held in selected middle schools. In New York, The Children's Aid Society's various community centers serve as recruitment sites. A team of AileyCamp staffers, male and female, conduct "mini-master class" presentations at each location and distribute applications. Following receipt of his or her application, each prospective camper is interviewed by a volunteer or staff member who has been trained in the interview process.

Although prospective campers are taught a simple dance routine as part of the recruitment presentations, proficiency in dance is not a requisite for admission, for AileyCamp in not a dance training program for talented students. The selection process certainly is designed to identify students who have an interest in dance or movement, including athletics; however, it is only one of many factors used in selection. AileyCamp targets children from lower socio-economic backgrounds identified as having one or more of the following at-risk factors:

- living with a single parent or no parent
- having a sibling who has dropped out of school or become a school-aged parent
- having difficulty with the traditional school structure as determined by teacher observation
- having low self-esteem

An ongoing program to follow AileyCamp is essential in order to reinforce and continue the process initiated at the camp. Two ways of extending the program's impact are through camp reunions, and a program of placement effort.

Camp reunions ideally occur every three months and include attending performances of dance and related arts, social time and refreshments, a motivational talk by a visiting AAADC artist and a time for campers to share their unfolding life experiences. In Baltimore, a relationship has been established with the University of Maryland, to hold monthly reunions from October through March with university students serving as mentors to the campers. The Western Maryland "mini-campers" attended a performance of the Alvin Ailey Repertory Ensemble at Frostburg State University in the fall of 1994.

In terms of program placement, New York's AileyCampers are already involved in Children's Aid Society activities in their neighborhood community centers, and the Alvin Ailey American Dance Center offers a minimum of two scholarships to CAS/AileyCampers who show promise.

Campers have commented on their experiences in glowing terms:

"What I really liked was the support and appreciation that we gave one another."

"I feel that AileyCamp was a great experience for me. It helped me to learn about other people's backgrounds and cultures as well as mine."

"AileyCamp taught me a lot about myself. I have more confidence as a result of this program. Best summer I ever had!"

". . . We learned styles of dance, famous dancers, choreographers, and directors. We got the inspiration that dance is different in many ways. It inspired some of us to take the audition [to study at the AAADC]. It taught us to focus and not to fall into the traps of wrong doings."

Parents also gave AileyCamp high marks. When asked if there were changes in their children's behavior and school performance as a result of the summer experience, they unanimously responded positively:

"His attitude and selfishness have changed for the better."

"Realizes it's hurtful and wrong to tease or put others down, and that it's wrong to fight; that they should talk out conflicts."

"She has become more responsible in her homework. Her grades have improved."

"Her attitude towards school has improved a great deal. She seems to be a little more involved."

One of the most exciting aspects of AileyCamp is the universality of its impact. The camp was originally designed to target youth from urban areas such as Baltimore and New York, but with the implementation of the mini-camp at Frostburg State University, it has been demonstrated that AileyCamp is also relevant and uniquely informative to young people from rural regions. Ailey-Camp's techniques of using dance as a vehicle for change and providing role models for success are enhanced by the cultural make up of the staff. The mini-camp director and the two dance instructors were black; the creative dramatics teacher was of Greek descent, and the guidance counselor was a native of the Frostburg area who had spent many years living in South America. A good number of the campers at Frostburg had only seen African Americans on television; at AileyCamp they were in positions of responsibility. A guest performance by the Washington Korean Dance Company provided the opportunity of a lifetime: the chance to speak and dance with a "real, live" Korean person. The campers rushed to greet the Koreans when they arrived on campus, helping to carry equipment, costumes, *anything* to participate in and contribute to this particular cultural exchange.

The mission of AileyCamp is a significant one. It is the mission to educate, enrich, and enliven the hearts of youth who must grapple daily with the severe realities of life. It is the mission to provide the children with an atmosphere of warmth, trust, and respect so that they can give free rein to their unique capabilities. It is the mission to realize Ailey's dream of touching all strata of society through the language of dance. It is a mission we will tackle each year at AileyCamp now and far into the future.

**Figure 25**   Maurice Curry leading a tap class at the CAS/AileyCamp, summer 1991. Photo by Bill Schropp.

*Choreography and Dance*, 1996, Vol 4(1), pp. 47–54
Photocopying permitted by license only

# Amazing Truth

Jennifer Dunning

What is the magic of Alvin Ailey's *Revelations* that keeps audiences filling the theater? The skill, the craft, the musicality and ultimately the spirit and the truthfulness of his choreography are examined. The body of Ailey's work fits into three general categories: abstract evocations of music; intensely emotional dances which are responses to social issues; and choreography celebrating the gifts and personalities of specific dancers. Examples of each of these categories are explored through such works as *Masekela Langage*, *Night Creature*, and *Revelations*.

KEY WORDS  *Revelations, Masekela Langage, Night Creature*, choreography, Black artists

Born dirt poor in rural Texas and raised by a troubled but beautiful and singularly imaginative mother, Alvin Ailey was a modern dance choreographer and company director of international renown by the time of his death, in 1989. These are the bare but crucial facts of his life. From them grew an extraordinary though somewhat underappreciated body of work that, like the life, in part defines what it is to be an American artist.

Ailey's life, like that of many American artists, was a peculiar and precarious balance of optimism and pessimism: always new frontiers; always a place farther west to mine gold; learning by doing and by ingenuity; calloused, dirt-ingrained hands to shame us before manicured Europeans. In Ailey's case, there was also the fact of being a black man with ideas, a sophisticated appreciation of the arts and a gift for making dances. And he came to prominence in an era when there was a growing acceptance of black artists, combined with lingering doubts (on the part of blacks as well as whites) about the validity of their accomplishments.

Ailey had plunged naively into his first, literature-driven choreography for Lester Horton's modern dance company in Los Angeles, pushed by Horton's sudden death and the company's need for new choreography. Soon after, Ailey came east, rediscovering the potency of his exotic good looks and virile physicality as he moved from solo dancer in the Broadway musical *House of Flowers* to a lead role in a Broadway play, *Tiger Tiger Burning Bright*, in six tumultuously crowded years. He was everywhere and knew everyone, it seemed, from Broadway to Harlem and south to the heated art and social scene of the 1960's in Greenwich Village. Ailey's timing was fortuitous, for black artists in all disciplines were speaking louder and being heard with new interest.

He was, however, a dancer first and foremost. That realization may have been underscored by important developments in his life. Acting on Broadway had been a difficult and even painful experience for Ailey, but he was offered a warm artistic home at the YWCA's new and adventurous little Clark Center in the theater district, where surrogate mothers and sisters, both black and white, loved and pushed him forward with the kind of uncompromising belief once provided by his own mother. It was at Clark Center that he put together a small professional company. For many years the dancers would gather there to board airport buses for the international tours that kept the company going. And it was at Clark Center that he refined his first two hit dances, the 1958 *Blues Suite* and *Revelations*, created in 1960.

Ailey lived life to the fullest, no matter how shabby or confused that life might be at times. Like many fundamentally shy and insecure people, he made a point of simply being himself, loud and clear, effectively raising a protective curtain of seeming transparency. He continued to learn the craft of choreography as he worked, as he had from Horton, Jack Cole and Broadway, learning from peers like Talley Beatty and Donald McKayle, at a time when they were establishing the necessary but eventually troublesome notion of "black" concert dance.

All of that went into his choreography. *Blues Suite* and *Revelations* were filled with the vital truth of a lucky – and gifted – beginner's outpourings of all he knew and had lived and cared about. And with the exception of a few ventures into pure abstraction that friends and close colleagues tended to dismiss as too "balletic," Ailey's experiencing of the world around him is the motive that drives his best choreography.

In all his work there is an underlying musicality and craft. His dances were often pushed into being by music. Pages and pages of cryptic notes on musical counts, carefully written out on long, yellow legal-pad pages, are to be found in the Ailey archives in Kansas City. There are also poetic notes on characters, vivid ideas for dances and costumes, and stage directions. Structure was important to him as well, and he had an apparently natural sense of how to put steps together to move a dance along. People who worked with him backstage early in his career in New York were astonished by his professionalism and efficiency. Unlike many of the fledgling choreographers creating their first programs at the Ninety-second Street Y, he knew what he wanted and knew how to communicate that clearly and without rancor when mistakes were made.

But Ailey was handicapped by a profound sense of failure and inadequacy. Trying, always, to make things better, he exasperated colleagues close to him with his inability to let go of choreography. They watched in pain, from benches in the rehearsal studio, as sequences of simple, elegant beauty became ornamented and theatricalized.

He had had only two years of concentrated technical training in dance, grabbed for the most part between periods of college study, a fact that would alone have made his achievements astounding. He loved to perform but also feared it from the start in Horton's tiny, protean theater. And nothing, he knew, would ever measure up to *Revelations* in the eyes of the public and his critics.

*Cry*, his celebration of Judith Jamison, his mother and all black women, came close to that success. And although it has continued to serve as a fascinating measure of talent as new generations of performers dance it, the solo itself looks more and more like a hypertheatrical, even shallow, *pièce d'occasion*.

The body of Ailey's work is far more substantial, fitting into three general, frequently overlapping categories that help to define his gifts. First, there is the choreography that is primarily an abstract evocation or response to a composer or a particular score.[1] Second, there are intensely emotional dances that respond to

---

[1]   Representatives of the first category of Ailey choreography include *The River, Mary Lou's Mass, The Lark Ascending, Night Creature, Isba* and *Escapades*.

social issues, many of which deal with the depredations of fame.[2] And there are the dances that seem to exist simply to express life's joys and sorrows and human foibles, bursting like ripe fruit with their juiciness. These include the two first classics, *Blues Suite* and *Revelations, Quintet, The Mooche, For Bird – With Love* and choreography created to celebrate the gifts and personalities of specific dancers and friends, like *Cry, Love Songs* (for Dudley Williams) and *Memoria* (a tribute to Joyce Trisler).

Ultimately, it is that spirit that audiences have loved best about Ailey, an unusually public and well-loved choreographer. Perceived as a man of the people in spite of his rarified profession, he created a body of work that is almost invariably described, by a surprising range of people, as heart-touching. Love, laughter and anger were expressed without hide-saving irony by a man who wanted to share his art and by dancers chosen by that man for their individuality and immediacy on stage as well as for their dance skills.

That expressive tone was sometimes tawdrily theatrical and even occasionally obtuse. Ailey was haunted by the charge of commercialism that was frequently leveled against his dances, but it was not always off the mark. And the process of choreographing was often torture for him, particularly as the burdens of directing a world-class company and maintaining its established levels of accomplishment grew heavier. He was a world-class procrastinator and comic stories abound of pieces being finished almost minutes before they were danced on stage. Somehow he managed to put it all together in work that continues, often, to surprise, long after a first viewing.

Robert Greskovic, the New York critic and dance historian, talks of one such eye-opener, *Isba*. "It made me realize what an unshakeable lyrical artist he was," Greskovic says.[3] "Ailey bought into all the politically aware stuff. He was aware. But at a basic level, everything was removed from these ordinarinesses of everyday life.

"What I loved about it was that I found all this depth in an automatic-pilot piece, a piece that didn't have any of the red flags that say, 'here's Important,' 'here's Direction.' No one was going to call it a breakthrough piece, or hot. It was none of those things that make a masterpiece of the canon, but I couldn't dismiss it and I knew it wasn't dismissable. I realized what an amazingly truthful artist Ailey was."

That truth – and Ailey's skill at expressing it – is equally present in all three Ailey genres, from *Masekela Langage* to *Night Creature* to *Revelations*. The 1969 *Masekela Langage*, inspired by the music of the South African trumpet player Hugh Masekela, reflects the concerns of the time about alienation, violence and repression, as suffered by and perpetrated against black citizens. Ailey insisted on maintaining a racially integrated company, even in times when that position was not politic or in fashion within the company or in the outside world. But notes in the Ailey archives suggest that he was not immune to intense feelings of rage against whites, particularly in his increasingly paranoid days in the late 1970's, before his manic depression and substance abuse were diagnosed and treated. Yet *Masekela Langage* also reflects an extremely difficult time within the Ailey company

---

[2]   Among the dances in the second category are *Masekela Langage, Flowers, Au Bord du Precipice, Witness* and *Survivors*.

[3]   Conversation with the author, 1994.

itself, a time of bitter battles between Ailey and his dancers over what they perceived as his hostility and indifference toward them.

The piece is animated by strong and specific emotions. They explode with the force of dynamite in the last moments, when a man crashes into the dusty little roadhouse where *Masekela Langage* takes place and, mortally wounded, dies in a thrashing solo before its stunned habitues. But the work is also a dramatically well-structured series of solos and ensemble dances that reveal character and prevailing dis-ease that identifies the time and place.

Ailey began work on the piece by having his dancers move to Masekela's recorded music, at first in a dormitory lounge at Connecticut College, where, at the American Dance Festival, *Masekela Langage* received its premiere. Social and modern dance are thoroughly mixed here, the social dancing used as earth in which the seeds of characters and themes can grow and become expressed through modern dance.

**Figure 26**   The Alvin Ailey American Dance Theater in *Night Creature* by Alvin Ailey. The photograph was taken on the occasion of the company's twenty-fifth anniversary.

*Night Creature* began, as many Ailey dances did, as a pragmatic *pièce d'occasion.* Ailey had to create something that would work for a television special on Duke Ellington and an upcoming company festival of Ellington's music, as well as a training piece for members of a new, young, second troupe of dancers. A record of his early work on *Night Creature* exists – with a rare (and fascinating) performance by Ailey himself – in a private videotape of the television special.

The choreography, structure and staging changed a great deal by the time the dance was performed on the stage of the New York State Theater during the 1974 Ellington Festival. Some of the material also appears in fairly undiluted form in *The River*, which Ailey created in 1970 for American Ballet Theatre. But, true to his great gifts for personalizing dance, there was in the shimmering stage crosses and impudent, ardent encounters of the pure-dance *Night Creature* all the youthful spirit of its original cast and the bittersweet playfulness and yearning of the Ellington score.

Both *Masekela Langage* and *Night Creature* are potent evocations of a moment in time and of the people who lived it, expressed in choreography and theater that are a good deal more sophisticated than much of *Revelations*. But neither of the later pieces can guarantee a full house as *Revelations* did, to Ailey's growing disgust late in his life. There were times when the dance seemed an albatross, a bit of bait that had to be thrown regularly into the hungry mouths of audiences to keep them happy. Ticket sales suffered when the classic was not on the program.

What is the magic of *Revelations*? It is simple and direct, but so is Doris Humphrey's *Day on Earth*, with its story of a man, a woman and their child moving with gentle inexorability through the life cycle. *Revelations* is theatrical, but so, certainly, is Ailey's *Blues Suite*. *Revelations* addresses the life of the spirit – in hope and in despair – like José Limón's powerful *Missa Brevis*. And *Revelations* is hugely enjoyable fun, but so are any number of dances by Paul Taylor.

**Figure 27** ''Processional'' section of Ailey's *Revelations* with Dudley Williams, Lucinda Ransom and Takako Asakawa.

The spirituals to which *Revelations* is danced do have a powerful, primal appeal, though Ves Harper, an early costume designer for that and other Ailey dances, was struck by the plain beauty of the choreography when it had to be danced without music in a performance on tour in Burma in the 1960's. There is in the songs, and in the choreography and scenic designs for the dance, a subtle interplay and juxtaposition of complexity and simplicity.

Most of all, however, *Revelations* was and remains the work of a community that is both general and specific, from the larger worlds of black Americans and those of all colors who believe and hope in something beyond themselves to the worlds of the individual dancers who helped create *Revelations* and passed it on to other generations. Like much of Ailey's early career, the dance was lucky in its timing, born in a gathering storm of social change and growing with those who lived through the changes. It was created (and refined over a period of about four years in the early 1960's) for a devoted band of friends, men and women whose professional lives were, in effect, a work of hopeful activism. Ailey was never one for hanging out with his dancers. His life with them was in the studio and on the stage. But the atmosphere in those early rehearsals was one of love and excitement.

The final, polished version of *Revelations* continued to change, of course, as its interpreters did. Ailey retired from performing and was able to scrutinize the piece from a clearer distance. His company became a very large, very successful institution. A growing audience for the art began to expect "big" dance. And the emphasis in performing shifted from dramatic expression to polished technique, with a corresponding loss in nuance. Music played live for dance, breathing extra life and experience into it, became an expensive thing of the past. And yet *Revelations* lives on, exerting its hold on audiences and the dancers who perform it.

Ailey borrowed from the world, a habit he certainly shared with other choreographers and cheerfully acknowledged. In McKayle's *They Call Her Moses*, a dance about Harriet Tubman created the same year as *Revelations*, Alvin danced a solo called "Run Brother Run" that McKayle suggests may have been an inspiration for the "Sinner Man" trio in *Revelations*. Carrying a child on his shoulders, Ailey crossed a billowing river on his knees, possibly suggesting to him the image of the three contrite sinners skidding across the stage on their knees, or even reinforcing or planting an idea for the baptismal scene in the piece. On an earlier visit to Los Angeles, in 1958, he saw a dance by James Truitte that was set to spirituals and that ended, as does *Revelations*, with "Elijah Rock." And at the time he was working on *Revelations*, Ailey collaborated with the director Vinette Carroll on *Dark of the Moon*, a folk play, set to spirituals, for which he created the dances.

*Revelations* was also fed by its earliest dancers. Pressed for time and eager to see their presence in the choreography, Ailey often pushed the dancers he trusted most to rework or even create parts of the choreography, which was then filtered through his own sensibility in rehearsal. Truitte, by then a company member, recalls that late one night in 1962, just before the company was scheduled to leave for the Jacob's Pillow Dance Festival, Ailey prevailed on him to create a solo drawn from his Horton technique, to be incorporated in a performance of *Revelations* for the television show "Lamp Unto My Feet."[4]

That solo was "I Want to Be Ready," one of the most haunting dances in *Revelations*. When Truitte later taught the prayerful, yearning solo to Dudley Williams, the younger performer reworked it with a substantial infusion of the Martha Graham technique that he had studied. Each man and each technique are powerfully present in the solo. And yet it retains its integrity, changing very little as witnessed by filmed archival material made before and after Williams took on the role.

*Revelations* has been called dancer-proof. Ailey did worry that newer, younger dancers, on hearing the applause the piece invariably gets, would be convinced that their performances were perfect. He worried that they could not understand its soul, coming as they did from a world so different from that of the dancers for whom it was created. But one way or another, the piece does get under the skin of its performers. Veteran *Revelations* dancers talk of how, surprisingly, the dance seldom seems a chore to perform, no matter how many times it is scheduled in a season. And the piece seems largely impervious to its interpreters' greater or lesser technical or dramatic skills, though it has gradually become more stylized. *Revelations* is a rich receptacle of living company history.

"There have been days when I've thought, 'Oh, God, not *Rev*,'" Williams said in a 1993 interview. "I had to wake up and look for new flavors." He'd ask Ailey if he could tinker a little. Try it, Ailey said, and he'd let Williams know if he felt it worked. And then there was no Ailey.

"Now that Alvin is gone, and so many people are gone, when I dance *Revelations* I bring somebody on stage with me," Williams says. "Somebody who has passed away. I bring that person on stage, and I dance with that person. I had a lot of friends who have passed away. And they have helped me in my growing. My only way of giving back to them is I take a name. It's almost like taking a name out of a hat. And I bring them on stage."

*Revelations* was a longer, rougher suite of dance and musical numbers in its first version, which Ailey described in program notes as a work that explored the "motivations and emotions of Negro religious music." That version was as much music as dance, grouped in three sections from which have remained "I been 'buked," a virtual abstraction of the dance as a whole and its themes, "Wade in the Water" and the church service finale, rooted in Ailey's memories of the Texas church services of his youth. Even so, that early mix, and Ailey's sure theatricality even then, stunned the first audience which greeted the frightened dancers with a total silence as the curtain fell, then burst out with startling cheers and screams as they stepped forward for their first how.

Early observers suggest that the potency of *Revelations* lies in Ailey's realization, whether conscious or not, that dance alone was the medium through which he could speak, as he needed to, from the heart. He was learning to do that in *Blues Suite*, and the process continued in *Revelations*. And that public education would continue, compellingly, for the rest of Ailey's career.

The success of *Revelations* had to do as much with an emotional truth that was its core, more clearly than in any other Ailey dance, as with its artistic values. The piece worked in part because it was a first glowing triumph in an artist's life, a

---

[4]   Conversation with the author, 1993.

work in which he says everything he needs to say with a freshness, innocence and ease he will never again possess. But most of Ailey's best dances are illumined to some extent by the glow of battles won, whether over personal devils or crushing external forces. While it is not within the reach of most of us to create with bold theatricality or choreographic complexity, we all understand what it means to struggle on.

To start, Ailey managed to complete *Masekela Langage* and *Night Creature* in spite of boiling personal pressures. But he also found a core of truth and expressed it clearly: about cruelty, and about Ellington, his music and his world. The young boy who had scribbled his thoughts on page after page of ruled pads he carried everywhere with him in Texas days now wrote those thoughts large, on a stage full of bodies, for everyone to share.

"Some choreographers are chess manipulators," Charles Blackwell, Ailey's first stage manager and an important influence in his early career, says.[5] "And there's nothing wrong with that. Chess is a nice game. But Alvin excited the body fluids.

"His things were about people. This, in another choreographer, might be a wave or an earth movement. But with Alvin it was a man and a woman reaching out. It was people. Everything was in the service of the emotions that he was dancing, or choreographing. It was not about showing off. It was always about what was being said. It was about tears, and perspiration, just reproduction. Mankind continuing."

---

[5]   Conversation with the author, 1993.

*Choreography and Dance*, 1996, Vol 4(1), pp. 55–58
Photocopying permitted by license only

# Eulogies

David Dinkins, Carmen de Lavallade, Judith Jamison, Maya Angelou

The following are eulogies delivered at the ceremony celebrating the life of Alvin Ailey, which took place at St. John The Divine Cathedral shortly after his death.

## Honorable David Dinkins, Mayor of New York City:

The death of Alvin Ailey, a brilliant, highly original creative artist is an indescribable loss not only for our city's cultural community, but indeed for the lovers of dance everywhere, since Alvin Ailey's art was in fact international in its scope and majesty.

To Alvin, the African American experience was solidly rooted in and inseparable from its American context. He mined that rich experience as no one had before him, constantly refining it in the crucible of his art and drawing from it the most essential elements which he then shaped into fine and lasting jewels.

## Carmen de Lavallade, friend and colleague, distinguished actress and dancer:

One of the unique things that Alvin brought to dance was his way of bringing everybody into the theater. It became popular theater; it was accessible to people. Concert dancing was always thought of as high brow or long hair. I think Alvin broke that pattern. Ordinary people, people who had never been to a concert before, realized it was for them, too. It really wasn't that austere or that forebidding; it made them feel welcome in a theater. It became very popular all over the world, no matter where he went. His language was universal. Everybody identified with it, Even when we were in South East Asia and Burma and places like that, people loved his work. *Loved his work*. He must have touched some part of their soul somewhere, a universal soul.

It is fitting that we give the last farewell here, because he was very much like this cathedral: lofty, wise, airy, strong because it is made of stone. Yet, at the same time, he had the delicacy and vulnerability of the stained glass windows, those tiny little fragments of light, so easy to break but yet so strong.

We come here as stone and as delicate glass. He took that strength and he built a legacy, a legacy for the young. I would like to pass that legacy on for Alvin. Don't let it go by. He gave you this gigantic chest, an open chest of gems and jewels and all you have to do – *And all you have to do* – is dip your hand in and take. You take and you use and then you pass on as we are passing on now. And it's up to the young people to take and use it, to pass it on, to support each other, not selfishly, but generously as Alvin has. And that's my heart to Alvin, and my words from him to you, the young people. We have done our job; now it's up to you to take it and lead, so that the dream and beauty live. And Alvin will always be on your shoulder to say, "Well done." And I say, "Well done, brother."

## Judith Jamison, Ailey's successor as Artistic Director of the Alvin Ailey American Dance Theater:

First time I ever saw Mr. Ailey was in 1963 in Philadelphia. He was on the stage, a little heavy, doing "Wading in the Water" and all of "Sinner Man." I saw this company who moved the way I hadn't seen before and a man who moved like a cat, who moved like quicksilver, who moved like an unearthly human being.

My relationship with Alvin was not one of words but of heartbeats and guidance. His hands knew my pulse through warm ups and work outs, when the heart was pumping life into those newly stretched and extended limbs. Through backstage butterflies, when the blood in my veins was mostly adrenalin and sweat. Through gratification and growth and wonder.

My mentor, Alvin Ailey, was my spiritual walker and support. He gave me legs until I could stand on my own as a dancer and as a choreographer. He was a spiritual walker, a poem poser, barefoot and bodytalker, servant salver and wader in the water. His life was a poem without words in an improvised meter, seldom heard but always heartfelt. A Zen Baptist master, his mantra was any movement repeated until it could be performed to perfection and often in defiance of gravity. But the revelations when they came were always worth the wait, the hard work and the long study.

He made us believe we could fly and many who came to see us soared with us as well, vicariously, viscerally with every lift and leap across the stage. Alvin lifted our spirits and transformed us. And the process of discovery for the dancer was always an adventure.

And what Alvin has left me with is an understanding that life brings love and hate, joy and pain, laughter, tears, trials, lies, truth and beauty, ugliness, hope and despair, rude awakenings and nice surprises, forgetfulness, memories and visions, revelations, illusion and disappointments, accolades and embarrassment, humiliation, innocence, experience and change.

But death makes all things precious. God rest and bless my spiritual walker.

## Maya Angelou, Pulitzer prize winning novelist and poet:
## For Alvin Ailey

When great trees fall
Rocks on distant hills shudder
Lions hunker down in tall grasses
And even elephants lumber after safety.

When great trees fall
Small things recoil into silence

Their senses eroded beyond fear.
They have, on hell hot days in lost gone years,
Stood beneath the branching
Secreted from the sun's probing fingers
Sheltered away from the sky's pelting downpour.

When great souls die
The air around us becomes light, rare, sterile.
We breath briefly, our eyes see briefly
With a hurtful clarity.
Our memory, suddenly sharpened
Gnaws on kind words unsaid
Promised walks never taken.

Great souls die and our reality
Bound to them, takes leave of us.
Our souls, dependant upon their nurture,
Now shrink, wisened
Our minds formed and informed
By their radiance, fly away.
We are not so maddened as much as
Reduced to the unutterable ignorance
Of dark, cold caves.

Yet when great souls die
After a period, peace blooms.
Slowly and always irregularly
Spaces fill with a kind of soothing vibration
Our senses restored, never to be the same of course
Whisper to us
They existed
They existed
We can be
Be and be better
Be and grow free
Be, for they existed.

Lord help us.
Give a look at him
Don't make him dress up in no nightgowns, Lord
Don't put no fuss and feathers on his shoulders, Lord
Let him know it's truly heaven
Let him keep his hat
His desk and everything
Let him have spats and canes
And Lord
Give him all the pliés he needs into eternity.

**Figure 28**   Alvin Ailey. Photo by Bob Greene.

*Choreography and Dance*, 1996, Vol 4(1), pp. 59–64
Photocopying permitted by license only

# Appendix I

## Alvin Ailey American Dance Theater Repertory from 1958–1993

| Year (World Premiere) | Choreographer | Ballet | Composer | Decor | Costumes | Lighting |
|---|---|---|---|---|---|---|
| 1958 | Alvin Ailey | Ode and Homage | Peggy Glanville-Hicks | Nomand Maxon | Nomand Maxon | Nicola Cernovitch |
| | Alvin Ailey | Blues Suite | Traditional Folk | Nomand Maxon | Nomand Maxon | Nicola Cernovitch |
| 1959 | Alvin Ailey | Ariette Oubliée | Claude Debussy | Nomand Maxon | Nomand Maxon | Nicola Cernovitch |
| | Alvin Ailey | Cinco Latinos | Traditional | – | Nomand Maxon | Nicola Cernovitch |
| | Alvin Ailey | Sanera | Alejandro Caturia | – | Thomas Wendland | Nicola Cernovitch |
| 1960 | Alvin Ailey | Revelations | Traditional | Ves Harper | Ves Harper | Nicola Cernovitch |
| | Alvin Ailey | Gillespiana | Lalo Schifrin | Ves Harper | Ves Harper | Nicola Cernovitch |
| | John Butler | Letter to a Lady | Ravel | – | John Butler | – |
| | Lester Horton | Variegatrons | John Wilson | – | – | Nicola Cernovitch |
| 1961 | Alvin Ailey | Knoxville Summer of 1915 | Samuel Barber | – | Joop Stoksis | Nicola Cernovitch |
| | Alvin Ailey | Creation of the World (New Version) | Darius Milhaud | Ves Harper | Ves Harper | Nicola Cernovitch |
| | Alvin Ailey | Three for Now–Modern Jazz Suite | Lalo Schifrin | – | – | – |
| | Alvin Ailey | Roots of the Blues | Traditional | Ves Harper | Ves Harpet | Nicola Cernovitch |
| | Alvin Ailey | Hermit Songs | Samuel Barber | – | Ves Harper | Nicola Cernovitch |
| 1962 | Alvin Ailey | Been Here and Gone | Traditional Folk | – | Ves Harper | Nicola Cernovitch |
| | Alvin Ailey | Reflections in D | Duke Ellington | – | – | Nicola Cernovitch |
| | Glen Tetley | Mountainway Chant | Carlos Chavez | Jac Venza | Jac Venza | Nicola Cernovitch |
| 1963 | Alvin Ailey | Labyrinth | Lawrence Rosenthal | – | Ves Harper | Nicola Cernovitch |
| | Alvin Ailey | Rivers, Streams, Doors | Traditional Folk | – | Ves Harper | Ves Harper |
| | Alvin Ailey | First Negro Centennial – Light – The Blues Ain't – My Mother, My Father | Duke Ellington | – | Ves Harper | – |
| 1964 | Alvin Ailey | The Twelve Gates | Traditional Folk | Geoffrey Holder | Geoffrey Holder | – |
| [1960] | Talley Beatty | Toccata | Lalo Schifrin | – | Matthew Cameron | Nicola Cernovitch |
| [1960] | Talley Beatty | Congo Tango Palace | Ellington/Strayhom | – | Matthew Cameron | Nicola Cernovitch |
| [1958] | Talley Beatty | The Road of the Phoebe Snow | Ellington/Strayhom | – | Normand Maxon | Chenault Spence |
| [1959] | Lester Horton | To José Clemente Orozco (from Dedications in Our Time) | Kenneth Klauss | Lester Horton | Lester Horton | Nicola Cernovitch |

| Year (World Premiere) | Choreographer | Ballet | Composer | Decor | Costumes | Lighting |
|---|---|---|---|---|---|---|
| [1947] | Lester Horton | The Beloved | Judith Hamilton | Lester Horton | Lester Horton | Nicola Cernovitch |
| [1955] | Anna Sokolow | Rooms | Kenyan Hopkins | - | - | Nicola Cernovitch |
| [1958] | Joyce Trisler | Journey | Charles Ives | - | Malcolm McCormick | Nicola Cernovitch |
| [1953] | Louis Johnson | Lament | Heitor Villa-Lobos | - | Matthew Cameron | Nicola Cernovitch |
| [1964] | Paul Sanasardo | Metallics | Henk Badings, Henry Cowell | Paul Sanasardo | Paul Sanasardo | Chenault Spence |
| [1960] | Talley Beatty | Come and Get the Beauty of it Hot | Mingus, Davis, & Schifrin | Talley Beatty | Matthew Cameron | Nicola Cernovitch |
| 1967 | Alvin Ailey | Riedaiglia | George Riedel | - | Alvin Ailey | Nicola Cernovitch |
|  | Talley Beatty | The Black Belt | Duke Ellington | Talley Beatty | Edward Burbridge | - |
| 1968 | Alvin Ailey | Quintet | Laura Nyro | - | Matthew Cameron | Nicola Cernovtch |
|  | Geoffrey Holder | The Prodigal Prince | Geoffrey Holder | Geoffrey Holder | Geoffrey Holder | Jim Housley |
| [1964] | Lucas Hoving | Icarus | Shin Ichi Matsushita | - | Beni Montrassor | Nicola Cernovitch |
|  | Robert Schwartz | Scrum | Various | - | - | - |
| 1969 | Alvin Ailey | Masekela Langage | Hugh Masekala | William Hammond | A. Christina Giannini | Chenault Spence |
|  | Pauline Koner | Poeme | Samuel Barber | Pauline Koner | A. Christina Giannini | Gene Lowery |
|  | Michael Smuin | Panambi | Alberto Ginaster | - | Marcos Paredes | Jim Housley |
|  | Joyce Trisler | Dance For Six | Antonio Vivaldi | - | Joyce Trisler | - |
|  | Richard Wagner | Threnodies | Tadeusz Baird | - | Lar Lubovitch | Lar Lubovitch |
| 1970 | Alvin Ailey | Streams | Milostav Kabelac | - | - | Chenault Spence |
|  | Alvin Ailey | Gymnopedies | Eric Satie | - | - | Chenault Spence |
|  | Miguel Godreau | Paz | Traditional | - | Rolando | Donovan Gray |
| [1964] | Geoffrey Holder | Adagio for a Dead Soldier | Tomaso Albinoni | - | Geoffrey Holder | Harold Armstrong/Ernest Baxter |
|  | John Parks | Black Unionism | John Coltrane | - | Judy Dearing | - |
|  | Kelvin Rotardier | The Cageling | Nat Adderly | - | Kelvin Rotardier | Donovan Gray |
|  | Kelvin Rotardier | Child of the Earth | Hugh Masekela | - | Kelvin Rotardier | Chenault Spence |
| 1971 | Alvin Ailey. | Flowers | Various | A. Christina Giannini | A. Christina Giannini | Nicola Cernovitch |
|  | Alvin Ailey | Archipelago | Andre Boucourechliev | - | A. Christina Giannini | Nicola Cernovitch |
|  | Alvin Ailey | Choral Dances | Benjamin Britten | - | A. Christina Giannini | Nicola Cernovitch |
|  | Alvin Ailey | Cry | Various Contemporary | - | - | Chenault Spence |
|  | Alvin Ailey | Mary Lou's Mass | Mary Lou Williams | - | A. Christina Giannini | Thomas Skelton |
|  | Alvin Ailey | Myth | Igor Stravinsky | - | A. Christina Giannini | Chenault Spence |
| [1962] | Brian McDonald | Time Out of Mind | Paul Creston | - | Rouben Ter-Arutunian | Chenault Spence |
|  | May O'Donnell | Suspension | Ray Green | Larry Ellaner | Charlotte Trowbridge | Chenault Spence |

| Year (World Premiere) | Choreographer | Ballet | Composer | Decor | Costumes | Lighting |
|---|---|---|---|---|---|---|
| 1972 | Alvin Ailey | The Lark Ascending | Ralph Vaughn Williams | — | Bea Feitler | Chenault Spence |
| | Alvin Ailey | Shaken Angels | Various(Rock) | Christian Holder | A. Christina Giannini | Chenault Spence |
| | Alvin Ailey | Love Songs | Various | — | Ursula Read | Shirley Prendergast |
| | John Butler | According to Eve | George Crumb | Rouben Ter-Arutunian | Rouben Ter-Arutunian | Nicola Cernovitch |
| [1943] | Katherine Dunham | Choros | Vadico Gogliano | — | John Pratt | Chenault Spence |
| [1959] | Donald McKayle | Rainbow 'Round My Shoulder | Traditional | — | Ursula Read | Chenault Spence |
| | John Parks | Nubian Lady | K. Barron | — | Judy Dearing | Shirley Prendergast |
| [1935] | Ted Shawn | Kinetic Molpai | Jess Meeker | — | Ted Shawn | Chenault Spence |
| 1973 | Alvin Ailey | Hidden Rites | Patrice Sciortina | — | Bea Feitler | Chenault Spence |
| [1959] | John Butler | Carmina Burana | Carl Orff | Paul Sylbert | Ruth Marley | Thomas Skelton |
| | Marlene Furtick | How Long Have It Been | Lightin Hopkins | — | Stephen Chandler | Shirley Prendergast |
| [1958] | José Limón | Missa Brevis | Zoltan Kodaly | — | Ming Cho Lee | Thomas De Gaetani |
| | Norman Walker | Clear Songs After Rain | Lou Harrison | — | Norman Walker | F. Mitchell Dena |
| 1974 | Alvin Ailey | Such Sweet Thunder | Duke Ellington | — | Randy Barcelo | Chenault Spence |
| | Alvin Ailey | Night Creature | Duke Ellington | — | Jane Greenwood | Chenault Spence |
| | Alvin Ailey | The Mooche | Duke Ellington | — | Randy Barcelo | |
| | Alvin Ailey | The Blues Ain't | Duke Ellington | — | Randy Barcelo | |
| | Alvin Ailey | Sonnet for Caesar | Duke Ellington | — | Jane Greenwood | |
| | Alvin Ailey | Sacred Concert | Duke Ellington | — | Jane Greenwood | |
| [1956] | John Butler | After Eden | Lee Hoiby | Irving Milton Duke | Rouben Ter-Arutunian | Shirley Prendergast |
| | John Butler | Portrait of Billie | Various | — | Normand Maxon | Shirley Prendergast |
| | Janet Collins | Canticle of the Elements | J S Bach/Heitor Villa-Lobos | — | Janet Collins | Chenault Spence |
| | Janet Collins | Spirituals | Traditional | — | Janet Collins | Chenault Spence |
| | John Jones | Nocturne | Yusaf Lateef | James Richards | John Jones | Chenault Spence |
| [1949] | Pearl Primus | Fanga | Traditional | — | Nancy Polls | Shirley Prendergast |
| [1961] | Pearl Primus | The Wedding | Traditional | — | Nancy Polls | Shirley Prendergast |
| 1975 | Milton Myers | Echoes in Blue | Duke Ellington | Salvatore Tagliarino | Normand Maxon | William Burd |
| [1952] | Lester Horton | Liberian Suite | Duke Ellington | — | Salvatore Tagliarino | Thomas Skelton |
| 1976 | Alvin Ailey | Black, Brown & Beige | Duke Ellington | — | Randy Barcelo | Chenault Spence |
| | Alvin Ailey | Pas de Duke | Duke Ellington | Rouben Ter-Arutunian | Rouben Ter-Arutunian | Chenault Spence |
| | Alvin Ailey | Three Black Kings | Duke & Mercer Ellington | — | Normand Maxon | Chenault Spence |
| | John Butler | Facets | Various | Irving Milton Duke | Jane Greenwood | Thomas Skelton |
| [1971] | George Faison | Gazelle | Various | Irving Milton Duke | George Faison | Shirley Prendergast |
| | George Faison | Hobo Sapiens | Stevie Wonder & Billy Preston | William Katz | George Faison | Shirley Prendergast |
| | Louis Falco | Caravan | Duke Ellington/Kamen | Vittorio Capece | William Katz | Richard Nelson |
| | Donald McKayle | Blood Memories | Howard Roberts | — | Hugh Sherrer | Chenault Spence |

| Year (World Premiere) | Choreographer | Ballet | Composer | Decor | Costumes | Lighting |
|---|---|---|---|---|---|---|
| 1977 [1971] | George Faison | Suite Otis | Various/Otis Redding | – | George Faison | Chenault Spence |
| [1972] | Lar Lubovitch | The Time Before The Time After (After the Time Before) | Igor Stravinsky | – | Priamo Espaitlat | Chenault Spence |
|  | Diane McIntyre | Ancestral Voices | Cecil Taylor | Romare Bearden | Romare Bearden | John D. Dodd |
|  | Jennifer Muller | Crossword | Burt Alcantara | Randy Barcelo | Randy Barcelo | Richard Nelson |
|  | Milton Myers | The Wait | Antonio Vivaldi | – | Duane Talley | Chenault Spence |
| [1966] | Rudy Perez | Countdown | Songs of the Auvergne | – | Rudy Perez | Chenault Spence |
| [1966] | Rudy Perez | Coverage II | Various | – | Rudy Perez | Chenault Spence |
| 1978 | Alvin Ailey | Passage | Hale Smith | Romare Bearden | Normand Maxon | Chenault Spence |
| [1974] | Rael Lamb | Butterfly | Morton Subotnik | – | Lawrence Watson | Chenault Spence |
|  | Eleo Pomare | Blood Burning Moon | Lateef, Ellington | A. Christina Giannini | Judy Dearing | Jennifer Tipton |
| 1979 | Alvin Ailey | Memoria | Keith Jarret | – | A. Christina Giannini | Chenault Spence |
| [1976] | Lar Lubovitch | Les Noces | Igor Stravinsky | – | Ann de Velder | Craig Miller |
| [1975] | George Faison | Tilt | Various | George Faison | George Faison | Jeffrey Schisser/ Nicola Cernovitch |
|  | Donald McKayle | District Storyville | Dorothea Freitag | Normand Maxon | Normand Maxon | Nicola Cernovitch |
| 1980 | Alvin Ailey | Phases | Various | – | A. Christina Giannini | Chenault Spence |
|  | Ulysses Dove | Inside | Robert Ruggieri | – | Judy Dearing | Craig Miller |
|  | Kathryn Posin | Later That Day | Philip Glass | A. Christina Giannini | A. Christina Giannini | Chenault Spence |
|  | Todd Bolander | The Still Point | Claude Debussy | – | Stanley Simmons | Chenault Spence |
| 1981 | Alvin Ailey | The River | Duke Ellington | – | A. Christina Giannini | Chenault Spence |
|  | Alvin Ailey | Landscape | Bela Bartok | – | A. Christina Giannini | Chenault Spence |
|  | Alvin Ailey | Spell | Keith Jarret | – | Randy Barcelo | Chenault Spence |
|  | Elisa Monte | Treading | Steve Reich | – | Marisol | Beverly Emmons |
|  | Billy Wilson | Concerto in F | George Gershwin | – | – | Chenault Spence |
|  | William Chaison | Places | Johann Sebastian Bach | – | William Chaison | Chenault Spence |
|  | Choo San Goh | Spectrum | Johann Sebastian Bach | Carol Vollet Garner | Carol Vollet Garner | Tony Tucci |
|  | Louis Johnson | Fontessa & Friends | Various | Edward Burbridge | Louis Johnson | Chenault Spence |
| 1982 | Elisa Monte | Pigs & Fishes | Glenn Branca | – | Elisa Monte | Craig Miller |
|  | Rodney Griffin | Sonnets | John Dowland | – | A. Christina Giannini | Chenault Spence |
|  | Alvin Ailey | Satyriade | Maurice Ravel | Carol Vollet Garner | Carol Vollet Garner | Chenault Spence |
| 1983 | Talley Beatty | The Stack-Up | Earth, Wind & Fire Two Tons of Fun Fearless Four Alphonse Mouson Grover Washington Jr. | adapted from a painting by Romare Bearden | Carol Vollet Garner | Chenault Spence |

| Year (World Premiere) | Choreographer | Ballet | Composer | Decor | Costumes | Lighting |
|---|---|---|---|---|---|---|
| 1983 | Bill T. Jones | Fever Swamp | Peter Gordon | Bill Katz | Bill Katz | Rick Nelson |
| | Gary DeLoatch | Research | Earl Klugh | – | Carol Vollet Garner | Thomas Skelton |
| | John Butler | Seven Journeys | Penderecki, Britten, Ruggieri | Tom John | Carol Vollet Garner | Chenault Spence |
| | Talley Beatty | Blueshift | Various Contemporary | Romare Bearden | Carol Vollet Garner | Chenault Spence |
| | Billy Wilson | Lullabye for a Jazz Baby | Arthur Cunningham & Talit Rasul Hakim | Carol Vollet Garner | Carol Vollet Garner | Chenault Spence |
| 1984 | Alvin Ailey | For "Bird" – With Love | Charlie Parker, Dizzy Gilliespie, Count Basie, Jerome Kern & Coleridge Taylor Perkinson | Randy Barcelo | Randy Barcelo | Timothy Hunter |
| | Alvin Ailey | Isba | George Winston | – | Jean Gonzales | Chenault Spence |
| | Loris Anthony Beckles | Anjour | Keith Jarret | Darryl Clegg | Lea Vivante | Beverly Emmons |
| | Donald McKayle | Collage | L. Subramaniam | – | Masazumi Chaya | Chenault Spence |
| | Judith Jamison | Divining | Kimati Dinizuluk & Monte Ellison | | | |
| [1983] | Alvin Ailey | Precipice | Pat Methany & Lyle Mays | Carol Vollet Garner | Carol Vollet Garner | Chenault Spence |
| 1985 | Bill T. Jones & Arnie Zane | How To Walk Like An Elephant | Conlon Nancarrow | – | William Katz | Beverly Emmons |
| [1982] | Ulysses Dove | Night Shade | Steve Reich | Ulysses Dove | Carol Vollet Garner | Timothy Hunter |
| [1974] | Jennifer Muller | Speeds | Burt Alacantara | – | Susan Hilferty & Jennifer Muller | Timothy Hunter |
| 1986 | Alvin Ailey | Survivors | Max Roach | Douglas Grekin | Toni Leslie James | Timothy Hunter |
| | Alvin Ailey | Caverna Magica | Andreas Vollenweider | Carot Vollet Garner | Carol Vollet Garner | Timothy Hunter |
| | Alvin Ailey | Witness | Traditional sung by Jessye Norman | Douglas Grekin & Patrick Venn | Kirsten Lund Nielson | Timothy Hunter |
| [1984] | Ulysses Dove | Bad Blood | Laurie Anderson | Carol Vollet Garner | Carol Vollet Garner | Beverly Emmons |
| 1987 | Katherine Dunham | The Magic of Katherine Dunham | Numerous Composers | John Pratt | John Pratt | Timothy Hunter |
| [1986] | Ulysses Dove | Vespers | Mikel Rouse | – | – | William H. Grant III |

| Year (World Premiere) | Choreographer | Ballet | Composer | Decor | Costumes | Lighting |
|---|---|---|---|---|---|---|
| 1988 | Rovars Deon | From the Mountains of Taubula | The Winans | – | Susan Gomez | Cynthia Caulfield |
| | Alvin Ailey | Opus McShann | Jay McShann & Others | Randy Barcelo | Randy Barcelo | Timothy Hunter |
| | Donald Byrd | Shards | Mio Morales | – | Gabriel Berry | Blu |
| | Kelvin Rotardier | Tell It Like It is | Terry Callier | – | Susan Gomez | Cynthia Caulfield |
| 1989 | Barry Martin | Chelsea's Bells | Robert Ruggieri & Melissa Etheridge | Duke Durfee | Monty Harris | Peter Fanelli |
| [1950] | Ulysses Dove | Episodes | Robert Ruggieri | – | Jorge Gallardo | John B. Read |
| | Lester Horton | Sarong Paramaribo | Les Baxter | – | José Coronado | – |
| 1990 [1989] | Judith Jamison | Forgotten Time | Le Mystere des Voix Bulgares | – | Judith Jamison & Ellen Mahika | Timothy Hunter |
| [1951] | Donald McKayle | Games | Traditional | William Burd | Remy Charlip | Chenault Spence |
| [1987] | Lar Lubovitch | North Star | Philip Glass | – | Clovis Ruffin | Craig Miller |
| [1988] | Kris World | Read Mathew 11:28 | Bobby McFerrin | – | Charles Schoonmaker | Timothy Hunter |
| 1991 | Donald Byrd | Dance At The Gym | Mio Morales | – | Davis Church | David H. Rosenburg |
| [1981] | Louis Falco | Escargot | Ralph MacDonald | – | Jeck Brusca | Richard Nelson |
| | Judith Jamison | Rift | Nona Hendryx | – | Kathryn Simon | Timothy Hunter |
| 1992 | Donald Byrd | A Folk Dance | Mio Morales | – | Gabrielle Perry | David H. Rosenburg |
| | Dwight Rhoden | Frames | Various Contemporary | – | Emilio Sosa | Daniel Bonitsky |
| | Billy Wilson | The Winter of Lisbon | Dizzy Gillespie | – | Barbara Forbes | Chenault Spence |
| [1988] | Jawole Willa Jo Zollar | Shelter | Junior Wedderburn | – | Terri Cousar | Meg Fox |
| 1993 | Judith Jamison (Libretto: Anna Deavere Smith) | Hymn | Robert Ruggieri | – | Joyce Anderson | Timothy Hunter |
| | Garth Fagan | Jukebox for Alvin | Antonin Dvorak. Taj Mahal, Keith Jarrett, Sly Dunbar & Robbie Shakespear | – | Carld Jorel Jonassaint | C.T. Oakes |
| [1958] | Jerome Robbins | N.Y. Export, Op. Jazz | Robert Prince | Ben Shahn | Ben Shahn & Florence Klotz | Jennifer Tipton |
| 1994 | Elisa Monte | Mnemonic Verses | Jon Hassell (Hassell) | Barbara Forbes | Mark Mongold | |
| | Brenda Way | Scissors Paper Stone | John "Mighty Mouth" Moschitta, John Lee Hooker, Loudon Wainwright III, Jimi Hendrix | Eleanor Coppola | Alex Nicols | |

*Choreography and Dance*, 1996, Vol 4(1), pp. 65–66
Photocopying permitted by license only

# Appendix II

### Alvin Ailey Repertory Ensemble
### Repertory from 1974–1994

| Choreographer | Ballet | Composer |
| --- | --- | --- |
| Gus Solomons, Jr. | Forty | Duke Ellington |
| Christine Lawson | Still Life | Duke Ellington |
| Milton Myers | Echoes in Blue | Duke Ellington |
| Raymond Sawyer | Afro–Eurasian Eclipse | Duke Ellington |
| Dianne McIntyre | Deep South Suite | Duke Ellington |
| Alvin McDuffie | New Orleans Junction | Duke Ellington |
| Donald McKayle | Games | Traditional Childrens Games |
| Donald McKayle | Vever | Coleridge Taylor Perkinson |
| Marlene Furtick | How Long Have It Been | Lightin Hopkins |
| Talley Beatty | Celebration | Earth Wind and Fire |
| Talley Beatty | Congo Tango Palace | Miles Davis |
| Talley Beatty | The Road of The Phoebe Snow | Duke Ellington, Billy Strayhorn |
| Lucas Hoving | Icarus | Shin Ichi Matsushita |
| Ulysses Dove | I See The Moon, and The Moon Sees Me | Robert Ruggeri |
| Mari Kajiwara | Interim | William Schuman |
| Judith Dejean | Des Amours Insolites Ou Les Duex S'en Melent | Chaconne Vitale |
| Billy Gornel | Colony | Vangelis/Oshra |
| Loris Anthony Beckles | Bridgeforms | Robert Pollock |
| Loris Anthony Beckles | Shanibello | Edward Grieg |
| Donald Byrd | Crumble | Cameo/Sound Design Beo and Mio |
| Louis Johnson | Workout | Contemporary/ Taped Collage |
| Bebe Miller | Cracklin' Blue | Patsy Cline/Bob Willis |
| Ralph Lemon | Folkdance | Ludwig Van Beethoven |
| Blondell Cummings | Basic Strategies IV | Michael Riesman Text-Blondell Cummings, Ralph Lemon |
| Kathryn Posin | Hunger and Thirst | David Borden |
| Kathryn Posin | New Works | Nana Vasconcelos |
| Kevin Wynn | Guerilla Love Song Dances | Joseph Reiser |
| Kevin Wynn | Nanigizmo | Gary Gibbs/Gayle Turner |
| Kevin Jeff | Seeds | Adam Randolph/ Bobby Hutcherson |
| Estelle Spurlock | Two In One | Stanton Davis |
| Eleo Pornare | Hex | Harry Partch |
| Eleo Pornare | Plague | Tape Collage |

| Choreographer | Ballet | Composer |
| --- | --- | --- |
| Smith and Shapiro | *To Have and To Hold* | Scott Killian |
|  | *3 Dances With Army Blankets* | Toby Twining |
| Keith Lee | *Exodus* | Bob Marley |
| Judith Jamison | *Tease* | Tape Collage |
| Penny Frank | *In Excelis* | Johann Sebastian Bach |
| Penny Frank | *Between Shadows* | Bela Bartok |
| Takako Asakawa | *Aria Animee* | Claude DeBussey |
| Ze'eva Cohen | *Summer Dance I,* | Mel Graves |
|  | *Summer Dance II* |  |
| Mary Barnett | *Migration* | Oregon |
| Fred Benjamin | *Ice Fire* | Mettianey/Mays |
| Warren Spears | *Knudsen Variations* | Kenneth Knudsen |
| George Faison | *Tilt* | Taped Collage |
| George Faison | *Gazelle* | David Newman/Art Blakey |
|  |  | Yusef Lateef |
| Nicolas Rodriguez | *Interfearance* | Tibetan Theatric Choir Gyuto |
|  |  | Monks |
| Gary DeLoatch | *Un-Four-Gettable* | Lasanas Priestess/Donald Byrd |
| Gary Ellis Frazier | *Baby Child Born* | Valerie Simpson |
| Katherine Dunham | *Choros* | Vadico Goliano |
| Pauline Koner | *Solitary Songs* | Luciano Berio |
| Kelvin Rotardier | *Child of The Earth* | Hugh Masakela |
| William Louther | *Wo-Man* | George Quincey |
| Judith Willis | *Songs For Young Lovers* | Tape Collage |
| Sophie Maslow | *Folksay* | Traditional |
| Rodney Griffen | *I'm Inclined to Knock Music* | Wolfgang Amadeus Mozart |
| Ray Tadio | *In Peaceful Arms* | Michael Jones |
| Dwight Rhoden | *Heart Strings* | Laurie Anderson/ |
|  |  | David Beal |
|  |  | Shirley Horn/ |
|  |  | Michael Shrieve |
| Andre Tyson | *Toxic Tranquility/* | Joan Armatrading/ |
|  | *Embattled Spirit* | Eurymthmics |
|  |  | Bobby McFerrin |
| Alvin Ailey | *Escapades* | Max Roach |
|  | *Streams* | Miloslav Kabelac |
|  | *Blues Suite* | Traditional |
|  | *Revelations* | Traditional |
|  | *Reflection in D* | Duke Ellington |
|  | *Isba* | George Winston |
|  | *Night Creature* | Duke Ellington |
|  | *MYTH* | Igor Stravinsky |

*Choreography and Dance*, 1996, Vol 4(1), pp. 67–68
Photocopying permitted by license only

# Notes on Contributors

**Allan S. Gray II** is the founder and Chairman Emeritus of the Kansas City Friends of Alvin Ailey and served for four years as Vice Chairman of the [Alvin Ailey] Dance Theater Foundation. Mr. Gray has also been intimately involved with the arts in a variety of other capacities: as a member of the Missouri Arts Council; a National Endowment for the Arts Panelist; and numerous arts organizations' Boards of Directors. He is a recipient of the Governor's Arts Award, the highest award presented by the state of Missouri, for his outstanding and lasting achievements.

**C. S'thembile West,** a performing arts critic, historian, dancer and educator, has a Ph.D. degree in African American Studies from Temple University. She has danced with the Chuck Davis Dance Company, Dianne McIntyre's Sounds in Motion Dance Company and Crowsfeet Dance Collective. She has taught dance and African American Studies at the City University of New York, Temple University and Bryn Mawr College. Ms. West has written for *The Philadelphia Enquirer, Attitude: The Dancer's Magazine,* and many other publications.

**Denise Jefferson** was born in Chicago where she studied ballet with Edna McRae. Upon moving to New York City, she received a scholarship to study at the Martha Graham Center for Contemporary Dance. While earning her Master of Arts degree in French from New York University, she became a member of the Pearl Lang Dance Company. In 1974, she joined the faculty of the Alvin Ailey American Dance Center, where she chaired the Graham-based modern dance department and served as Scholarship Director. She has taught at: Benedict College; New York University's Tisch School of the Arts; Phildanco; American Dance Festival; and as a guest teacher at the Bat-Dor School in Israel; London Contemporary Dance School; National Dance Theatre of Bermuda and the International Summer Dance Academy in Cologne, Germany. Ms. Jefferson serves as a member of the Dance Panel of the New York State Council on the Arts, the Commission on Accreditation of the National Association of Schools of Dance and as Vice Chairman of the International Association for Blacks in Dance. Ms. Jefferson was appointed Director of the Alvin Ailey American Dance Center in 1984.

**James Truitte** was a principle dancer with the Lester Horton Dance Theatre and an original member of the Alvin Ailey American Dance Theater in which he was a principal dancer and Associate Artistic Director. He has appeared in all media: movies, television and concert stage, and has been Artist In Residence with the Dayton Contemporary Dance Company since 1976. Mr. Truitte has taught extensively throughout the United States and in Europe and Australia in schools, universities and companies and has received many awards for excellence. He is recognized as the leading exponent of the Lester Horton Technique. In 1993 he was awarded the status of Professor Emeritus from the University of Cincinnati College Conservatory of Music, where he taught regularly for many years. Mr. Truitte continues as guest teacher, adjudicator, dance panelist and maintains close ties with the Dayton Contemporary Dance Company and Phildanco.

**Jennifer Dunning** has been a member of the dance staff of *The New York Times* since 1977. She wrote *But First A School*, a history of the School of American Ballet, and contributed to *L'Après-midi d'un faune*, a book of essays on the photography of Baron de Meyer, and *Saratoga*, a cultural and photographic history. She is writing a critical biography of Alvin Ailey.

**Muriel Topaz** is currently author and editor of the Young Dance section of *Dance Magazine*, and editorial consultant for Gordon and Breach publishers, with responsibility for the journal *Choreography and Dance*, and the book series *Choreography and Dance Studies*. She is active as a Notator and Reconstructor most recently having staged *Jardin Aux Lilas* (Tudor) for the Milwaukee Ballet, and *Continuo* for the Paris Conservatory, and having notated *Moor's Pavane* (Limón). She was Director of the Dance Division of the Juilliard School from 1985 to 1993, Executive Director of the Dance Notation Bureau from 1978 to 1985 and was the principle organizer and co-chair of both the First International Congress on Movement Notation in Israel and the Second in Hong Kong. Her distinguished career has included work as dancer, teacher, reconstructor, author, editor, Labanotator, dance panelist, adjudicator and board member for dance companies and organizations throughout the world.

**Ronnie Favors** began dancing as a child in her hometown of Iowa City, Iowa. After graduating from high school, she traveled to New York to study at the Alvin Ailey American Dance Center. Ms. Favors has been a member of the Alvin Ailey Repertory Ensemble, the Alvin Ailey American Dance Theater, and the Lar Lubovitch Dance Company as well as appearing in several music videos and television commercials. She was the ballet instructor at AileyCamp's 1989 inaugural year in Kansas City, and served as the Artistic Director there in 1990. Ms. Favors has been combining responsibilities as the AileyCamp Project Director and the Director of CAS/AileyCamp since 1991.

**Sylvia Waters** studied dance at the New Dance Group and later earned a Bachelor of Science degree in dance at The Juilliard School, where she studied with Antony Tudor and Martha Graham. She began her performing career with Donald McKayle's dance company. She spent several years in Paris where she appeared regularly in television and worked with Michele Descombé, then Director of the Paris Opera Ballet, Maurice Béjart and Milko Sparenbleck. Ms. Waters returned to the United States in 1968 and joined the Alvin Ailey American Dance Theater. She toured throughout the United States, South America, Europe and the Soviet Union as a principal dancer with the company until assuming her current position as Artistic Director of the Alvin Ailey Repertory Ensemble, a position she has held since the ensemble's inception in 1974.

*Choreography and Dance*, 1996, Vol 4(1), pp. 69–70
Photocopying permitted by license only

# Index

# CHOREOGRAPHY AND DANCE
## AN INTERNATIONAL JOURNAL

**Notes for contributors**

Submission of a paper will be taken to imply that it represents original work not previously published, that it is not being considered for publication elsewhere and that, if accepted for publication, it will not be published elsewhere in the same form, in any language, without the consent of editor and publisher. It is a condition of acceptance by the editor of a typescript for publication that the publisher automatically acquires the copyright of the typescript throughout the world. It will also be assumed that the author has obtained all necessary permissions to include in the paper items such as quotations, musical examples, figures, tables etc. Permissions should be paid for prior to submission.

**Typescripts**. Papers should be submitted in triplicate to the Editors, *Choreography and Dance*, c/o Harwood Academic Publishers, at:

| | | | | |
|---|---|---|---|---|
| 5th Floor, Reading Bridge House | | PO Box 32160 | | 3-14-9, Okubo |
| Reading Bridge Approach | | Newark | | Shinjuku-ku |
| Reading RG1 8PP | | NJ 07102 | | Tokyo 169-0072 |
| UK | or | USA | or | Japan |

Papers should be typed or word processed with double spacing on one side of good quality ISO A4 ($212 \times 297$ mm) paper with a 3 cm left-hand margin. Papers are accepted only in English.

**Abstracts and Keywords**. Each paper requires an abstract of 100–150 words summarizing the significant coverage and findings, presented on a separate sheet of paper. Abstracts should be followed by up to six key words or phrases which, between them, should indicate the subject matter of the paper. These will be used for indexing and data retrieval purposes.

**Figures**. All figures (photographs, schema, charts, diagrams and graphs) should be numbered with consecutive arabic numerals, have descriptive captions and be mentioned in the text. Figures should be kept separate from the text but an approximate position for each should be indicated in the margin of the typescript. It is the author's responsibility to obtain permission for any reproduction from other sources.

*Preparation*: Line drawings must be of a high enough standard for direct reproduction; photocopies are not acceptable. They should be prepared in black (india) ink on white art paper, card or tracing paper, with all the lettering and symbols included. Computer-generated graphics of a similar high quality are also acceptable, as are good sharp photoprints ("glossies"). Computer print-outs must be completely legible. Photographs intended for halftone reproduction must be good glossy original prints of maximum contrast. Redrawing or retouching of unusable figures will be charged to authors.

*Size*: Figures should be planned so that they reduce to 12 cm column width. The preferred width of line drawings is 24 cm, with capital lettering 4 mm high, for reduction by one-half. Photographs for halftone reproduction should be approximately twice the desired finished size.

*Captions*: A list of figure captions, with the relevant figure numbers, should be typed on a separate sheet of paper and included with the typescript.

*Musical examples*: Musical examples should be designated as "Figure 1" etc., and the recommendations above for preparation and sizing should be followed. Examples must be well prepared and of a high standard for reproduction, as they will not be redrawn or retouched by the printer.

In the case of large scores, musical examples will have to be reduced in size and so some clarity will be lost. This should be borne in mind especially with orchestral scores.

**Notes** are indicated by superior arabic numerals without parentheses. The text of the notes should be collected at the end of the paper.

**References** are indicated in the text by the name and date system either "Recent work (Smith & Jones, 1987, Robinson, 1985, 1987) ..." or "Recently Smith & Jones (1987) ..." If a publication has more than three authors, list all names on the first occurrence; on subsequent occurrences use the first author's name plus "*et al.*" Use an ampersand rather than "and" between the last two authors. If there is more than one publication by the same author(s) in the same year, distinguish by adding a, b, c etc. to both the text citation and the list of references (e.g. "Smith, 1986a"). References should be collected and typed in alphabetical order after the Notes and Acknowledgements sections (if these exist). Examples:

Benedetti, J. (1988) *Stanislavski*, London: Methuen.

Granville-Barker, H. (1934) Shakespeare's dramatic art. In *A Companion to Shakespeare Studies*, edited by H. Granville-Barker and G.B. Harrison, p. 84. Cambridge: Cambridge University Press.

Johnston, D. (1970) Policy in theatre. *Hibernia*, **16**, 16.

**Proofs.** Authors will receive page proofs (including figures) by air mail for correction and these must be returned as instructed within 48 hours of receipt. Please ensure that a full postal address is given on the first page of the typescript so that proofs are not delayed in the post. Authors' alterations, other than those of a typographical nature, in excess of 10% of the original composition cost, will be charged to authors.

**Page Charges.** There are no page charges to individuals or institutions.